Online Marketing
business using T'
other social netw

MW01165110

Online Marketing Help: How to promote your online business using Twitter, Facebook, MySpace and other social networks

David Amerland

Online Success Series

David Amerland

Copyright © David Amerland 2011. All rights reserved.

ISBN: 978-1-84481-988-1

The right of David Amerland to be identified as copyright holder
of this work has been asserted in accordance with the Copyright,
Designs and Patents Act, 1988. This ebook edition published
2010

Marketing Help: How to promote your online business using
Twitter, Facebook, MySpace and other social networks

Published by New Line Publishing, 118 Gatley Road, Cheadle,
Cheshire, SK8 4AD, UK.

This Book can be purchased in electronic format at:
www.helpmyseo.com and all major online eBook retailers
including Amazon and the Sony store.

Editing, cover and interior design by WebDirectStudio
www.webdirectstudio.com (website)
info@webdirectstudio.com (email)

Notice of Rights
All rights reserved. No part of this publication may be
reproduced, stored in a retrieval system, or transmitted, in any
form or by any means, electronic, mechanical, photocopying,
recording or otherwise, without the prior permission of both the
publishers and copyright owner.

This book is sold subject to the condition that it shall not, by way
of trade or otherwise, be lent, resold, hired out or otherwise
circulated without the publisher's prior consent in any form of
binding or cover other than that in which it is published and
without a similar condition including this condition being
imposed on the subsequent purchaser.

Limit of Liability / Disclaimer of Warranty

Online Success Series

Online Marketing Help: How to promote your online business using Twitter, Facebook, MySpace and other social networks.

Whilst the author and publisher have used their best efforts in preparing this publication, they make no representations of warranties with respect to the accuracy or completeness of its contents and specifically disclaim any implied warranties of merchantability or fitness for a particular purpose. No warranty may be created or extended by sales representatives or sales materials. The advice and strategies contained herein may not be suitable for your situation. You should consult with a professional where appropriate. Neither the author nor publisher shall be liable for the use or non-use of the information contained herein. The fact that a website or organization is referred to in this publication as a citation and/or potential source of further information does not mean that the author or publisher endorses the information that the website or organization may provide or recommendations it may make.

License
Purchase of this publication entitles the buyer to keep one copy on his or her computers (when in digital format) that are for personal use and to print out one copy only. The buyer is not permitted to electronically post it, install it or distribute it in a manner that allows access by others.

The scanning, uploading and distributing of this publication via the Internet, or via any other means, without the permission of the publisher, is illegal and punishable by law. Please purchase only authorized electronic editions, and do not participate or encourage electronic piracy of copyrighted materials. Your support of the author's rights is appreciated.

Online Success Series

David Amerland

Online Success Series

Online Marketing Help: How to promote your online business using Twitter, Facebook, MySpace and other social networks.

To all those who work online, here's to making it! And for N, thank you. You just make everything make sense.

David Amerland

Acknowledgments

No book is ever written in a vacuum. *Online Marketing Help* is the result of many people who commented on the effectiveness of each chapter. Too numerous to mention individually, to each of you I am more than grateful. Particular gratitude must go to WDS for their cover designs and StudioB for their unstinting support in all my writing.

Table of Contents

Introduction   **2**

Chapter #1 - What is the real time web?   **3**

Chapter #2 - How can the real time web help your business?   **11**

Chapter #3 - What are the applications of the real time web?   **25**

Chapter #4 - How to decide when to use the real time web   **49**

Chapter #5 - Understanding the strengths and weaknesses of Facebook   **63**

Chapter #6 - What else is there?   **77**

Chapter #7 - Going viral   **85**

Chapter #8 - Niche not mass   **97**

Chapter #9 - The year of SEO   **101**

Chapter #10 - The Last Word   **115**

Appendix 1 - How to ask effective questions on Twitter   **118**

Appendix 2 - How to create a Facebook profile page you can use to market your business   **121**

Appendix 3 - How to create a customized Facebook Fan Page   **126**

Appendix 4 - How to optimize video to rank high on search engines   **131**

Social Media Marketing: 101 Terms you need to know   **136**

Online Success Series

Introduction

On the web, marketing is, always, a process of a string of activities which when looked at individually differ little from 'playing around' online.

Over the last ten years we have seen a constant trend towards greater immediacy, interactivity and relevancy in just about everything the web stands for. For those who try to run a business and market it at the same time the challenge is huge.

To meet it adequately it requires more time than is usually available, more knowledge than is usually at hand, more expertise than can usually be reasonably tapped and the ability to think about it all in a way which is only possible if there was time (which there isn't) and the luxury of conceptual distance so that those working in their online business can start to work on their online business, instead.

This book goes some way towards addressing the inequalities and giving you the tools you need to succeed online. It is practical, written in plain English and designed to replace the expensive, knowledgeable, hired hand you would have hired had you had the cash available to do so.

I sincerely hope it helps you become more successful, competitive and visible online allowing you to enjoy more time and greater wealth.

David
Athens, 2011

Chapter #1
What is the real time web?

*Information is the oxygen of the modern age. It
seeps through the walls topped by barbed wire, it
wafts across the electrified borders.*
Ronald Reagan

In order to master anything we need to understand it
and this, usually, means grasping its strengths and
weaknesses and internalizing how each applies to
what we want to do with it.

The 'real time web' is a generic term applied to
technologies and practices which enable users to

---

receive information as soon as it is published by its authors, rather than requiring that they or their software check a source periodically for updates.

This is the official definition. To me, you, and anyone actively involved in online marketing the real time web is the ability to send out messages which have immediate marketing impact and, by the same token, receive messages which have immediate marketing value.

While this is new to us, now, it's not really new as a concept. Financial market traders, dealing in the highly volatile world of stocks and commodities have always lived in the real time web, even before the worldwide web was created.

Information is key. And information can vary from one moment to the next depending on many variables. The financial market is based upon fresh, real-time information because it has to make projections about the future.

Until we entered the 21st century we were conditioned to work on information which, at best, was days old and at worst weeks or even months old. Newspapers gave us 'news' which was 'new' to us but old in terms of when it happened, even when the paper was a daily one.

News gathering television services gave us 'news' which was, often, based on newspapers and, bizarrely for a live broadcast service, managed to actually be older in terms of the value of information it gave us than its paper-based cousins.

We accepted all this because, as individuals and unlike traders, we did not have the tools to access information ourselves. We were hostage, for lack of a better word, to the organizations which did have these tools and who, in their function of news gathering and news dissemination, acted as censors of sorts and guardians of information.

To be fair, the process to which these news gathering organizations were subject to was closely bound to their perception of what was (and is) important to us. In that respect, they were 'censors' only as far as our perceived needs and wants in terms of information allowed them to be.

There is a problem of course with this kind of model for news dissemination. First, it has natural boundaries. Newspapers have a finite number of pages and the place of each news item on each page is itself a form or prioritization of the importance of that piece of news. Television news programs have finite airing times; usually 30 minutes and the news have to be made to fit into that slot.

Second, in presenting us with what they think they know is relevant to us, news gathering organizations create an unwittingly eschewed view of the world. A view to which we are direct contributors because we project the perception of what we need, which news gathering organizations respond to.

This is far from perfect. We are rarely honest even to ourselves. Asked by a reporter what music I listen to, for instance, I will probably say Classical or The Scorpions, depending on the situation. In reality I listen to a lot more than that in a much greater variance than I could ever explain and for reasons which are intensely personal.

This light-hearted example perfectly showcases the issue of allowing any service apart from ourselves to serve news to us. We can end up believing that the whole world is exactly as we want to picture it. Great if we are independently wealthy and want nothing to bother our perfect lives. Not so great if we really need information in order to understand the world and successfully market to it.

We can, of course, always look for alternative ways of finding out about what's going on. We can choose to buy more than just one newspaper and we can listen to more than just one news service and we could, these days, visit more than one news website.

While this is certainly possible (and always has been) it does not solve the intractable problem of there being only 24 hours in any day and time, for us, is always finite. We can only, realistically, devote so much to working, researching and living and still maintain a balance which is healthy from a personal point of view.

So, in the world we've left behind, last century and, even, the opening years of our time, information; though technically free, was not immediately available. Instead, everything we saw and everything we heard was days, weeks, months old and any decision or choice we made based on it was already heading towards the moment in time when it would have to be revised again.

Traders and the real time flow of information

Those who work in banking and investments know that information is worth nothing if it's not in real time.

Their world is governed by the moment. Yesterday's news, to them, is dead and gone. Stocks and commodities, shares and the flow of money are always influenced by what is happening right now. This makes the world of the trader volatile, fluid and totally current. It is interesting to note that traders and banking influence the world we live in (and the global credit crunch is a perfect example of that). The only other form of 'business' outside banking which had (and continues to have) real time information is the military and we know that it also has immediate impact upon our world.

When you compare these two to almost every other form of trade or business or practice, which relies on delayed information we begin to see a relatively simple but powerful connection being made between the ability to have real time, unfiltered information and the quality of the decisions which can then be made.

This has a direct impact upon every business decision you make. Whether working offline or online the ability to access real time information and communicate in real time with your potential clients can make or break your business.

Last century this would have been an assertion which could have been laughed out of town. Last century things were different. The global economy was not as networked. The online population was not as large. The business market place was not as crowded.

Today the factors are different. Tactical advantage in the real world depends upon the ability a business has to communicate directly with its customers in real time. The flow of information here is bi-directional. Customers also want to be able to communicate with a particular business or a type of business in real time.

Just like for traders and bankers, the real time flow of information is necessary and works only if it pays off.

Traders know that unless they have real time information for commodities they will make decisions which will cost them money. The same applies for investment bankers working with stocks and shares. Real time information for them confers to an advantage in business (and profitability) which becomes the immediate pay-off.

It is no different to you, me and anyone else working (and partially living) online. Unless there is a real, tangible advantage to having and using real time information then there is little point in going through the trouble of getting it.

The entire point of this book is that real time information and the ability to communicate in real time with your potential customers does give you, exactly, the kind of advantage which is translated into profit for your business and helps you make strategic decisions which will ensure your ability to increase your market share.

Throughout this book I use the words 'strategic', 'market share' and 'tactical' in the same way they are used when developing strategy, battling for market share and looking to confer tactical advantages for large, national, or multi-national, corporate operations. The truth is, however, that the methodologies, processes and imperatives which affect a one-person business are no different except perhaps in scale.

If you are serious about succeeding in the online world today you need to be able to wear many hats and understand just what processes affect what you do.

To give you but one example, the marketing of my first book: *SEO Help: 20 steps to get your website to Google's #1 page* involved the use of real time communication every day for three months. Because I was busy with juggling several projects at once I did not follow my own marketing plan the first month.

In that month the book made just a little below 300 sales. As my schedule cleared I applied real time communication to my marketing, taking advantage of the opportunity to also communicate several time-sensitive SEO issues.

As a result the sales doubled every month for the four months that I was able to sustain the real time communication campaign.

There are two lessons to be learnt from my own example. First, if you are struggling for time you need to be realistic in what you can do and discipline yourself to do it. Second, there is direct value to be gained from real time communication which has immediate impact upon the bottom line.

On the web, today, we are all traders. The real time flow of information is what allows us to succeed in today's wired world and those who rely on the traditional time-lag of communications to make decisions and communicate with their customers, will, as we shall see, eventually fail.

Chapter #2

How can the real time web help your business?

Information is not knowledge.
Albert Einstein

I need to begin this chapter with an example and I am jumping the gun a little because we have not even looked at real time web tools. However it is necessary to do so first in order to frame some of the things which we will look at a little later on.

I live in a fashionable Manchester suburb where refined living has given greater value to activities which are normally considered so commonplace that they are not even remarked upon in other parts of the world.

Take fresh bread for instance. Like most people I get mine from a supermarket which also has a bakery. So the choice for me is packaged, sliced bread (a 20th century miracle) or fresh bread from the supermarket bakery which has been baked that day.

There is, of course, a third choice. My suburb has a bakery. It is relatively small, ran by two brothers and it bakes excellent bread and some of the best chocolate filled donuts this side of the Atlantic. While I love their bread the problem is that is always sells out quickly, they never can make enough and, because I lead a life as jam-packed with work as everybody else I know, I can never get to the bakery at a decent time. Because I happen to know one of the brothers I did mention this to them and they tried to have a regular time upon which they would bring out fresh bread.

As an experiment it failed because they could not manage all the different aspects of running a modern bakery so that they could always guarantee to bring out bread at the same, regular time. For most of their customers, just like me, this was catastrophic. There is nothing worse than driving out three miles, getting there, finding parking and then having to either wait an hour (disaster!) or finding out that you are an hour late and all the bread has sold out.

The bakery has a website. It also has a Twitter account to which I subscribe. This has been my lifeline. As one of the brothers Tweets when bread has gone in the oven and the time it will come out (and then Tweets again the moment it is out) I have, recently, managed to have fresh bread at home on most days of the week.

The brothers have also told me that fresh bread sales have increased in the year by 15% (at a time when it is a little more expensive than fresh supermarket bread) and they have managed to increase customer satisfaction (gauged by the increase in repeat business) by 12%.

Not bad when you consider that all this was achieved by a simple action which delivered real time information to those who needed it.

We shall go on here to examine just how real time information both transmitted and received can help your business grow but first let's look at an important point which was so rightly stated by Einstein.

The true value of information

There is a tendency, itself born out of sloppy thinking to confuse knowledge with information. These two are not the same though on rare occasions they might be interchangeable.

For the record, it is worth formally stating here that information is facts. Knowledge is analysis or, rather, what you do with the facts.

Because information is factual it is also, usually again, non-exclusive. A fact may break out now and you may be the first to get hold of it but others will follow. In that respect information is universally accessible. No matter how hard you try to contain it or try to restrict it, it will find a way to break free. Knowledge, on the other hand, is almost always proprietary. Unlike information knowledge does not simply 'become available' because it also is not volunteered easily.

The reason I am belaboring the point here is because the real time web is only useful if you get the information you need in order to generate knowledge. Information is the raw material, so to speak, out of which knowledge is manufactured.

The analogy is a good one. Like any manufacturing process the better the quality of your raw material happens to be the better the quality of the manufactured result is going to be. Similarly, with information, the better the quality of the information you receive happens to be, the better will be the knowledge which you will be able to manufacture from it.

Real time communication as a means of brand building

If you had a shop which sold something to customers you would want to spend as much time as possible talking to those who shop there.

There are good reasons for such an action:
1. You learn who they are and why they shop with you
2. You find out what they like and what they do not like

3. You get to find out what they need
4. You would talk to them in order to differentiate your business
5. You would talk to them so you can find out where else they shop and what they buy
6. You use then as a sounding board for offering new things

The applications of how you would use this are so many and the benefits so tangible that it is a no-brainer that the most personal of mediums, the web, would go in that direction the moment the technology which would allow it, developed.

The technology now has been developed to the point where the web can be used for real time communication and one of the principal applications of the practice has to do with brand both in terms of building a stronger brand presence and creating better brand awareness.

Having the ability to communicate in real time with your potential customers at next to no cost (barring time and effort) is an invaluable means of creating the kind of engagement and rapport necessary to lead to better positioning in the market.

Online Success Series

Real time communication as a means of increasing customer numbers

These days, numbers matter, irrespective of what you do or what you are at. I have a friend, called Alisa Miller, who writes non-fiction books and the occasional novel. She is a respected relationship counselor and author and has a website which attracts thousands each month. Her career as a writer and readership however only took off after she created a personal Facebook page. Her personal profile on Facebook is always full at the 5,000 friends mark but what really drives her brand and book sales is the fact that her Facebook fan page has over 20,000 fans who she interacts with on a daily basis and who actively seek out her writings.

To achieve this she is totally engaged in what she does with daily postings to her Twitter and Facebook accounts, discussions, whimsies as well as postings of more serious stuff.

There is a point to all this in that numbers is what creates success rather than the other way around. This gives you an idea of where we are heading with this.

In today's fast-paced world, there is so much information coming at us from everywhere that it becomes increasingly difficult to process it, never mind act on it. As a result most people fall back on the means of learning which have developed evolutionary: acquiring information through the interactions of our social network.

Social networks, however small or large may be in a real-world setting are always characterized by the fact that they tend to happen now. In the here and now the constraints prevent us from accessing information in any other way other than immediately which means that however much information we come across we tend to filter it the same way we filter news we hear when we are 'outside'.

In the real world the information which comes our way is assessed by us according to two main factors: First, who told us and secondly when we were told.

Who told us the information is important because we have been programmed by evolution to place a value on what we hear depending on our assessment of the trustworthiness of the person who does the telling. A piece of information coming from someone we know and trust, in our minds, becomes a lot more valuable than a piece of information we have come across ourselves, even if the former is pure opinion and the latter is fact-filled.

I know this sounds ridiculous. After all we want to believe that we are supremely rational and our decisions are based on logic. Unfortunately this is not so and I will give you an example. I recently bought a 4x4. It suits my lifestyle and it is something which I felt I needed to do before I get to the age where owning a 4x4 gets to be a joke in itself. Because I believe in the value of information I checked to see, carefully, the 4x4 vehicles available in my price range and then I went online and accessed several reviews on each one.

It was an admittedly lengthy process which, nonetheless, allowed me to arrive at one make of vehicle which according to the information I had would be perfect in terms of value, quality and performance and still fit within the amount of money I wanted to spend.

As it happens, towards the end of my selection process I happened to go out with a friend for a drink and, in passing, that evening I mentioned the make of car I was planning to buy. He said, "yeah, it's a really reliable car, you should be totally happy with it." I didn't ask him how he knew this nor did he offer any corroborative information, so in terms of what he said this was a purely subjective opinion.

Yet, months later, having bought the car, and being indeed very pleased with it, all I remember is not the reams and reams of reports and comparative details which I had painstakingly unearthed, downloaded and poured over, but my friend's passing remark.

Wiring is an issue. Although we operate in a world which moves at breakneck speed, where markets rise and dip within hours, responding to minutiae which change by the minute we are, still, conditioned to remember and respond to social interactions better than we do to cold, hard data.

This is one of the reasons why the real-time web and real-time social marketing are so powerful.

Because we do not biologically evolve at the same rapid pace as our technology we tend to behave online much as we offline. We, for example, use our social networking connections in exactly the same way in terms of getting and retaining information as we do our offline ones. News shared and information passed along, online, in a social network environment holds more weight than stuff we ferret out ourselves or we passively come across as part of our online research.

This made, in 2010, Facebook exceed Google as the main means of serving information and the fact itself became the catalyst Google needed to launch their core Google search engine update (called Google Caffeine) which took into account social marketing and a website's presence in the social networks as a metric of its search engine optimization (SEO) status.

What this means, for you and your plans to get your products and services promoted online is that unless you have a strategy in place about how to communicate with your intended audience you will be one of those hapless companies and individuals who get online and treat the real time web like a television channel where they need to blast an advert at a passive audience.

I will tell you straight away that this is a strategy which does not work. It will get you ignored (at best), absorb resources in terms of time and marketing which you can ill afford to lose and, unless you realise what you are doing wrong, will get you disheartened with real-time web marketing and leave you scratching your head as to what the fuss is all about.

This brings us squarely to the next part of this chapter which is just what kind of strategy should you have in the real time web, what 'strategy' means in the first place and, obviously, how to begin to formulate one.

Developing a real time web strategy

Mention the word 'strategy' in any context and you run the risk of being perceived as manipulative, nefarious and about as trustworthy as Enron's accountants.

In fact 'strategy' means planning which requires a process which itself is broken down into doable steps which then simply make it easier to implement as part of a daily routine. It sounds easy yet 40% of companies fail to have a real time web strategy in place and, according to ComScore[1], a web usage monitoring company, more than half of the companies in the marketplace fail to grasp the fundamental shift

---

[1] comScore, Inc. (NASDAQ: SCOR) is a global leader in measuring the digital world and preferred source of digital marketing intelligence. In an independent survey of 800 of the most influential publishers, advertising agencies and advertisers conducted by William Blair & Company in January 2009, comScore was rated the " most preferred online audience measurement service" by 50% of respondents, a full 25 points ahead of its nearest competitor. comScore's capabilities are based on a massive, global cross-section of approximately 2 million Internet users who have given comScore permission to confidentially capture their browsing and transaction behavior, including online and offline purchasing. comScore panelists also participate in survey research that gathers and integrates their attitudes and intentions. Using its proprietary technology, comScore measures what matters across a broad spectrum of digital behavior and attitudes, helping clients design more powerful marketing strategies that deliver superior ROI. With its recent acquisition of M:Metrics, comScore is also a leading source of data on mobile usage. comScore services are used by more than 1,200 clients, including global leaders such as AOL, Microsoft, Yahoo!, BBC, Carat, Cyworld, Deutsche Bank, France Telecom, Best Buy, The Newspaper Association of America, Financial Times, ESPN, Fox Sports, Nestle, Starcom, Universal McCann, the United States Postal Service, the University of Chicago, Verizon Services Group and ViaMichelin.

in communication required by the real time web and, as a result, either ignore it completely or pay lip-service to it without really intending to engage in any kind of real time web participatory model of communication.

Why?

One of the problems is inertia. Large companies and even many of the medium-sized ones have a certain degree of inertia in their decision-making process. The need for meetings, approvals and accountability in terms of implementation strategies means that it may be weeks and even months between the moment a meeting is called up to discuss a specific issue and the moment the system of communication discussed and agreed upon is ready to go into operation.

Another problem is accountability. Companies like to control their communication with their clients because it gives them a false sense of security. After all if all you put in place in terms of how you describe a product or service are the contents of the company's brochure then you can feel justifiably smug in having 'controlled' or 'managed' the company's public message and its image.

The real-time web requires a company to pass the responsibility for its image and the message it sends about its products from its own personnel into the hands of an unpaid army of fans, customers and potential customers. While the success of such strategy is every online marketer's dream, the reality of it fills every company CEO with dread.

Yet, fail to do this and in the vacuum created by your absence will step in exactly those who you fear and do not want to deal with in the first place. BP found this out in the most painful way possible when its leaking oil pipe in the Gulf of Mexico became the most talked about environmental disaster in Twitter.

With the company maintaining real-time web silence the ones who gained the most traction were those prepared to rubbish its environmental record, corporate response to a massive ecological disaster and inability to take into account the fears and pain of those directly affected by it.

Large companies and companies where those inside them are still governed by old world models of communication automatically mistrust the very tools which could help them steal a march on their competitors and manage to gain valuable publicity with very little money at a time when the small amount of money available is an issue in its own right which they need to face.

Those who do get it sometimes make the mistake of working it ad hoc as time allows, missing out, as a result, a valuable opportunity to gain a larger pie of the market.

All of this, of course, leads us to the first million dollar question of the book which is, what should you be looking at in terms of creating real time web content? Obviously the whole idea of a strategy is that you need to have a very specific approach to what you post online, when and where. So let's begin by saying that when it comes to posting content on the real time web you first have to begin with the 'how' rather than the 'what' and in order for this to be really effective you need to first understand the 'why'.

It is only be establishing specific targets and goals which will guide your activities in terms of what you are trying to accomplish that you will then be able to use content for specific purposes and have a means of measuring the effectiveness of what you are doing.

The next part of this book will help you understand what the applications of the real-time web are so that you can then establish targets which are realistic and explain how they can be measured so that you can put in place a coherent real-time web strategy.

01001101011000010110101101100101001000000011
11001011011110111010101110010001000000011011
11011011100110110001101001011011100110101 0
01000000110110101100001011100100110101101 10
01010111010001101001011011100110011100100 00
00111001101100001011100110111001101111001 00
10110000100000011001010110111001100111011 00
00101100111011010010110111001100111001000 00
01100001011011001100100001000000110010101 1
11000011000110110100101110100011010010110 11
100110011100100001

Chapter #3

What are the applications of the real time web?

We aren't in an information age, we are in an entertainment age.
Tony Robbins

In order to use anything correctly it is important to know, first, why we are using it. Information and the real time web are no exception. Let's begin with some of its more widely applicable uses which will help you to understand how it can be applied to you:

Online Success Series

1. Breaking news and background for media outlets - If something happens today somewhere on planet earth, it is often reported on Twitter first. Twitter is also the means through which much valuable information gets about in a way which allows it to be accessed immediately and promoted through a global network of unpaid online marketers.

2. Spreading important information
There might be times when it becomes necessary to spread information to either a large number of people (viral marketing in the real time web) or a specific group of people (subscription marketing in the real time web) very quickly. This is what my local bakery does, each time they bake fresh bread. This is where special offers, up-to-the-minute changes in trading hours and even management crisis efforts (like BP should have engaged in from moment one during the Mexican Gulf oil spill disaster) should be communicated.

3. Organizing events
The ability of the real time web to affect instant communication about events which can be acted upon immediately gives it real value in terms of organizing promotions and short-notice gatherings. This ranges from such promotional gimmicks like 'flash mobs' to real-value items such as sudden sales, tickets to an event which have suddenly become available and,

even, parties and impromptu gatherings. Again, the emphasis here is on information with a specific bias, sometimes 'entertaining' (i.e. the flash mob example) and at other times with a very practical bias (such as tickets to an opera or a football event or, even, a competition). How you use the ability the real-time web gives you to organize events depends upon the nature of your business and what you need to communicate to your clients.

4. Collective intelligence
It is true that the best allies you have for your business are your customers. In an ideal world you would like to take each of your customers aside and find out what they really want from your company. In terms of the time and effort required this is an unrealistic approach which no business can undertake, unless, of course, they know how to use the real-time web. Using real-time services you can actually engage your target audience in troubleshooting your services and products and even suggesting new directions you should be thinking of taking. This makes communication at this level an invaluable resource. It gives you the ability to make your business appear customer-friendly and transparent and it allows you to turn your customers into unpaid consultants, engaging them closely with your business all the while.

5. Social awareness
No 21st century firm which has no social awareness can hope to last long in the modern marketplace. Today's consumers demand much more than those

they spend their money with than a great product and perfect service. Companies today (even one-man ones) need to be engaged in the communities they operate in. Advertising that engagement however usually smacks of insincerity and capitalizing on it only makes you appear cynical. Real-time web announcements however allow you to get past that perception and benefit from the spontaneity and zest of a real-time announcement of an event or fact which illustrates your engagement with the community you trade in and, in addition, may even get you a mini-wave of viral marketing.

6. Market transparency

Go to Twingly Microblog search (http://www.twingly.com/microblogsearch), enter the name of any product, and you get a list of people's opinion about it. Customers use the tools of the real-time web to say what they think about brands and services. The results might not be sophisticated reviews like on specific websites made for product reviews, but aggregated and analyzed based on technologies for sentiment analysis, the results can be very helpful for others and at least provide an additional source of information right before a planned purchase. Under the assumption that there are the right tools for extracting the relevant feedback from the stream of status updates, the real-time web can increase the transparency of markets and give your new potential customers the confidence required to do business with you and your company and access your services.

7. Help customers find you based on their locations
People are always on the move and that is true for most of your customers. With the upcoming combination of real-time elements and location features – that even Twitter is taking seriously now – it will be pretty easy to connect with people being at any given location anywhere in the world. So someone who is interested in your products or services, in your area, will be able to find you easier than ever before. As a matter of fact the ability to have what is, to all intents and purposes, an up-to-date system of 'Yellow Pages' is of greater value to those outside the area, coming in, as it is their vey unfamiliarity with their surroundings which places you at an advantage when it comes to winning their custom, provided, of course, that they can find you fast and easily.

8. "Social" media
Everyone is using the term "Social Media" loosely to refer to a million different things and tools, but in this specific context, what we mean is that the real-time web makes existing media and media channels become a social experience. There are two trends which are converging here and they can produce a really powerful phenomenon. The first is connectivity. Everyone these days seems to have Twitter and Facebook on their smartphone and watch TV or be at the Cinema and still be connected to the web. The other is that the web has become the preferred stake out for many of us. We spend time

online sharing opinions, passing on products and services we find and seamlessly blending our time off work with our work interests. It is in this blurring of the two different time modes that the real-time web comes into its own, allowing for powerful, real-time, viral marketing which is the digital equivalent of the word-of-mouth publicity you could have down the pub, except that here the whole world gets to know about you and your services.

Understanding the true value of real time information

Those who do not 'get it' dismiss the advent of the real-time web as a gimmick which will pass. Yet an overview of trends on the web shows that we have, as a global population of users, being heading, since its inception, towards greater and greater degrees of immediacy and interaction.

There is a very specific reason why this trend has developed and why it will continue to play a vital role in the development of the web and this has to do with physiology, or rather the neurobiological aspect of our evolution which is our brains.

Whether we like it or not we have evolved in a way where there are reward centers in the brain which, when activated, make us feel good about ourselves, the world and everything in it.

The feeling is persistent enough and physiologically deep enough to actually have an impact on our behavior so that it escapes the boundaries of logic.

Drugs and drug addiction, for instance, have the ability to harm us and logically we should not be taking them. The fact that we do and the fact that we often cannot help ourselves has to do with the fact that drugs activate the same reward centers, albeit to a different degree, which the use of real time media does.

This in itself should be sufficient to help us realize that when it comes to the web the use of real time media as a means of communication and interaction is only going to increase, not decrease.

This is a book about using the real time web to better market your business rather than a volume analyzing the development dynamics of online behavior so focusing only on that you already know that whatever marketing decision you make requires, as a starting point, information.

Marketing is a funny business because it relies on trends and guesswork. Because it takes so much energy and money to put in place, it's at its most effective when it has correctly analyzed what's current and then correctly guessed what the next best thing is going to be and put out a message which addresses both.

Here I cannot guess exactly how complex your business is. You could be selling ice-cream to the masses or have developed a niche product which requires a specialized audience. The truth is however that we all live now in a global, intimately interconnected world. We have found out the hard way that a mortgage crisis in the United States has the ability to affect purchasing power in Australia and unemployment figures in the United Kingdom.

If you are really serious about your marketing (even if your online business consists of you, your dog and your pet parrot) you really need to apply the same kind of thinking and analysis to it as that applied by Coca Cola before they commit $100 million to their next campaign.

Coca Cola has (or buys in) analysts, planners and executives whose job is to get this right. Yet the very power of the web (and this book) is that you can achieve the same quality of analysis if you use the real time web properly and, in addition, act upon your decision with greater speed than a massive corporation, with its organizational inertia, could ever manage.

The practical applications of the real-time web From understanding what the global economy is doing (which will affect the purchasing power of your online visitors) to spotting trends and understanding what will happen next in the marketplace you are active in.

The best way to show how this is done is to use a couple of examples and then extrapolate from there into more practical applications.

Using the real time web to predict the future

If you had the ability to predict the future how much would this be worth to you?

I know this sounds little whimsical as a question (and I was toying with the idea of writing in a whole paragraph about a Hot Tub Time Machine) but I assure you it is anything but whimsical.

Apart from the obvious jokes regarding the lottery numbers and tomorrow's horse race results predicting the future is a need which has spawned a global multi-billion dollar industry the origins of which go back in time.

In antiquity self-respecting emperors and heads of state used to have their own seers, ready to cast the bones or read the omens in the sky for a sign of what was to come. The outcomes of epic battles and major political decisions were made based on information about the future.

In pre-history, in ancient Greece, the oracle of Delphi became a king-maker of sorts by playing exactly this role of predicting what was to come, albeit in a way which made every answer it gave appear to be true in retrospect, an approach which helped built its reputation and wealth).

Today we spend more not less money in modern-day seers who range from your local palm reader willing to tell you who you will eventually marry for the price of a take out to heavy-hitting business analysts who use an impressive array of expensive software to predict the stock market, business trends and the 'next hot thing'.

Predicting the future costs. Corporations and those individuals who invest hundreds of thousands or even millions, have no problem paying the exorbitant prices the industry's modern seers command.

If you are in that playing field and already have millions in the bank ready to invest I will tell you that whatever you are paying your business analysts is a total waste of time. Today we spend money for a little bit of reassurance not unlike those sought by emperors of the past before they launched a campaign of conquest.

In the late 1980's, investment author Burton G. Malkiel made waves in the financial community with his book *A Random Walk Down Wall Street*. The book was not so much an attack on stock brokers as it was an assault on the entire idea of actively managed investing. Using an impressive array of data and studies, Malkiel convincingly showed that most investors lack consistent skill at timing markets or picking winning stocks over the long-term.

His most controversial claim was that a monkey throwing wet paper towels at a stock chart on the wall could beat an expert armed with statistics and stock picking formulas. Intrigued (and no doubt annoyed) by this statement, the *Wall Street Journal* took it as a challenge and ran a simulated experiment where people threw darts at stock charts while experts picked stocks deliberately. While the dart throwers didn't win out (the experts got it right 61 out of 100 tries), the experiment did show the investing public that completely random dart tosses beat the experts 39% of the time.

What does this have to do with you, us and the real-time web? Plenty. The real-time web is an unprecedented analysis tool capable of showing what is currently hot (or developing) and allowing those with a little knowledge to accurately predict what is happening without having to spend a dime.

Here are two real-life examples: suppose you are closely following the election results between two major parties because, depending on the outcome a local project is likely to get funded or not and real estate prices in a particular area are going to rise.

Or you want to know which of this summer's movies is going to be a major success because you are printing out a line of T-shirts based on the concept. In most cases the results of both these examples, even with heavy investing in expert analysts, would be obvious only after the event. By then the information would not be especially privileged as anyone capable of reading a newspaper or watching the news on TV will know and whatever marketing advantage you were looking for will have evaporated.

I have taken Hollywood Blockbusters as an example because so much money rides on each one that there is, usually, a mini-industry which deals in predictions and springs up around each film.

On April 2010, researchers at Hewlett Packard turned their attention on Twitter as a means of predicting a film's success and its actual amount of takings in each weekend of showing based on the number of Twits and re-Twits which the micro-blogging site fielded. The result was nothing less than astonishing.

Their system predicted that zombie film *The Crazies* would take $16.8m in its first weekend in the US. It actually took $16.06m.

The team also forecast that the romantic drama *Dear John* would take $30.71m in its first US weekend. It took $30.46m.

The computer scientists at HP used a specifically written algorithm. But what is of note here is that they made use of information which is readily available to me and you and which can, even at a naked-eye level, give us a clear indication of what is happening, to make predictions which beat the finely honed Hollywood machine at its own game and uncover information which allowed them to make predictions which were based on much better data than anything Hollywood had managed to come up with.

The point is that the same kind of information which was available to the HP researchers is also available to us, for free. So for the time it takes to click a few times and check some details we can obtain the kind of information which corporations can't buy with their deep pockets.

Data mining Twitter for fun and profit

Let's, in the first instance, explore just how you can data mine Twitter in order to get the kind of information you need.

As you have probably guessed there are several ways and here we will examine each of them and its application.

Twitter Search: When you are first checking to see what is happening with a specific topic in Twitter your first point of call should be Twitter's own search engine: http://search.twitter.com/. Simply point your browser its way input the query and gauge how much interest there is from the Tweeting that's going on. If you are interested in, for instance, to discover how much my book on SEO titled *SEO Help: 20 search engine optimization steps to get your website to Google's #1 page* is doing you could try putting in "SEO Help book". If you are interested in seeing just how popular SEO is currently as a topic simply input SEO and see what comes up and who is Tweeting.

Twitter search is perfect for trending topics and for carrying out vanity searches for your name, products or website. Its immediacy gives you a snapshot of what people are talking about and its effectiveness is not unlike if you could eavesdrop in the conversations or thoughts of thousands of people at once.

Scanning RSS feeds: As each user on Twitter gets their own RSS feeds and Twitter itself generates a feed, being able to scan them through a process called Pipes gives you a tool as powerful in its reach and depth as any a corporation would like to have. To start a Pipe scan go to: http://pipes.yahoo.com/pipes/ and look at the Homepage video explaining how to create a Pipe. The process is simple enough for almost anyone to do, it requires no knowledge of coding whatsoever and its drag and drop approach enables you to build a Pipe of your choice in minutes. Using your Pipe you can search Twitter for any number of keyword phrases on the topic you are interested in and, best yet, by using an RSS Reader to run your Pipe through you do not even need to worry about visiting the site.

Checkout a Graphical representation: Analyzing an RSS feed and getting constant updates is pretty cool but it does feel a little geeky. When it comes to information, those of us who are true information junkies, it feels good to sometimes have some impressive looking graph to look at and imagine yourself in a plush boardroom on the 35th floor of a corporate tower, planning to take over the world. For that priceless CEO feel check out the Twitter Stream Graphs: http://www.neoformix.com/2008/TwitterStreamGraphs.html or the already created search on the site: http://www.neoformix.com/Projects/TwitterStreamGraphs/view.php. Twitter Stream Graphs is exactly what it says it is, a graphical representation of at least 1000 Tweets over one or two days giving you an instant visual picture of the trend for the topic you are looking for. If you are working for a company and you want to show your boss just how much volume you have generated in Twitter noise for a particular keyword then Twitter Stream Graphics is your tool for getting that promotion. It is also totally useful for comparing what's happening to a particular keyword in terms of interest across several days or weeks even. This kind of analysis gives you a powerful tool for predicting future trends and gauging interest in particular topics, ahead of the pack.

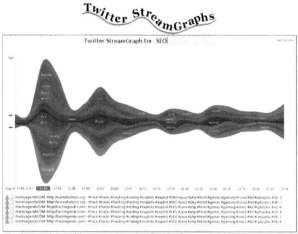

A quick search for 'SEO' gives me the trend for that topic.

Twitter Volume: Sometimes you may have to look for a number of different keywords, for example: 'SEO', 'SEO Help' and 'SEO Help Book'. When you carry out a search like that it helps to be able to compare the volume of mentions (or 'traffic') associated with each keyword as this can become a valuable strategic tool for determining what is happening and how to go about using the information you find out as a result. Tweet Volume (http://tweetvolume.com/) is perfect for carrying out such analysis and presenting it in a visual way which makes it easy to quantify and understand. In the case of the keywords I chose, for instance, I can see that

'SEO Help Book' generated over 19,000 mentions. The fact that 'SEO' generated, in that period, over 800,000 gives me an idea of the interest involved and the size of the potential market for my book, on Twitter.

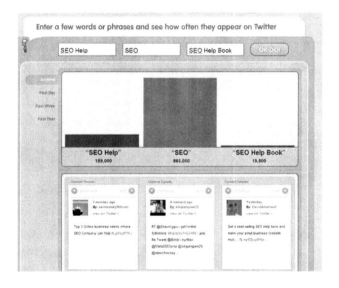

A quick search shows me the volume for each of my keywords.

Tweetminster & Peep Gov: There may well be times when politics is on the agenda and you really want to know what's happening across the political spectrum which may influence your business decisions. Tweetminster (http://tweetminster.co.uk/) trucks topics talked about by UK politicians, journalists,

MPs and bloggers and allows you to see what's happening in UK politics in real time. The equivalent site for US politics and the trending issues of interest there is Peep Gov (http://www.peepgov.com/). Regarding political postings and influence a site called WeFollow also allows you to see just how many followers politicians, political bloggers and political sites have on Twitter (http://wefollow.com/twitter/politics).

These are online tools for carrying out fast, in-depth monitoring of the single largest, micro-blogging site on the planet. Use them well and you will end up with a precise window into the real-time web, its trends and topics of interest, which will enable you to form a well-informed opinion about the subjects you are researching.

When it comes to making business or marketing decisions we are all only as good as the value of the information we have access to and, in this case, you have just been handed an arsenal of real-time information analysis tools which put you on a par with any large corporation.

Used correctly Twitter gives you the ability to globalize the way you would operate locally when you were looking to confirm a piece of information or get corroborative evidence of an opinion.

This becomes a powerful way to jump ahead of trends and get on bandwagons at the very beginning, when the going is good. It is also a powerful means to research anything which has to do directly with your business.

Twitter, although huge in terms of the number of users it has, is still only one site and because its main users tend to be tech-savvy, 20 to 30-somethings, the bulk of its demographics skews a little the picture your research gives you.

This is why we shall look at, next, how to explore other aspects of the real-time web, getting valuable information in real time, from a wider audience and more evenly distributed demographics.

Searching the real-time web for trends

If your business marketing and business development decisions are going to be based upon real-time web information then you need to have the best information possible.

If you are looking at a trend, for instance, about a particular issue which your product or service is going to answer you need to know if there is interest out there and just how much of it there is.

Apart from Twitter, real-time web news and interaction breaks out on sites which range from news aggregator Digg (www.digg.com) to Facebook (www.facebook.com) and the number of people who interact on them represent a sizeable portion of the viable online population which any service or product needs to target, in order to succeed.

The tools listed below are designed to take you past the limits of Twitter and provide you with further corroborative, valuable information.

OneRiot (http://www.oneriot.com/): OneRiot is a real-time web search engine which scans social networking websites to bring you the latest news from many of the major real-time web sites. Simply go to the website, type your search term in the query box there and see what the results are.

Google (http://www.google.com): The world's most successful search engine has not given up on real-time web search. Carry out your search as normal. In the example below I am looking for 'SEO Help book'

Now at the end of the Google search results URL manually add the following parameter: **&as_qdr=d** this has the result that it refines the Google search to results which are only 24 hours old. Google recently upgraded its search engine algorithm to speed up website indexing and the result is that many popular websites now find their content online just hours, instead of weeks, of having placed it online.

In our example, by adding **&as_qdr=d** manually to the end of the Google search URL of my search I get:

The result shows me that I really need to update my website: http://helpmyseo.com so that it shows up on the 24-hour search (it was on the results in the non-filtered example) and it also shows me just what is happening within the SEO field in the last 24 hours.

If you need to do real-time web searches frequently
and want to avoid the hassle of having to constantly
remember which code to add to the end of Google
search string URL then do the following trick:

Get Firefox as a browser (it can be downloaded from:
http://www.mozilla.com/en-US/firefox/firefox.html).
Once you have it set up, open the about:config page
in Firefox and replace the value of keyword.URL
variable with the following URL:
http://www.google.com/search?as_qdr=d&q=

Here's how to do it. Open up Firefox and in the
address bar window type about:config. You should
see the following notice:

Click on "I'll be careful, I promise". You will next
see a screen with a Filter field:

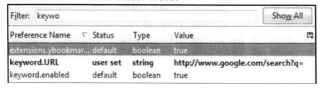

Type '**keyword.url**' in the Filter text box to locate keyword.url. Double click on '**keyword.url**'. Change the default value of **keyword.url** with:
http://www.google.com/search?as_qdr=d&q=
click 'OK' and that's it! From now on, when you use Firefox every search you run will go through Google's 24 hour filter and give you real-time web search results.

Scoopler (http://www.scoopler.com/): As the name suggests, Scoopler, is about getting a 'scoop'. It's a real-time search engine which looks at all the content people are sharing across real-time services like Twitter, Digg, Delicious, Flickr and other, popular social networking websites. It then ranks all this content by freshness, popularity and authority to continuously deliver the most up-to-date results available on the web. As a means of cross-referencing everything you find through other services it is truly invaluable.

Google Fast Flip (http://fastflip.googlelabs.com/): In the pre-web age if you were doing some research to find out what's hot so that you can the decide where to put your money or how to best shape your marketing you started either at the library or your local newsagent. Newspapers and magazines are still a valid point to start from as they reflect the views, interests and needs of a large segment of the population. Google Fast Flip is still in beta and a scan through it will show you if your thoughts and ideas are heading in the right direction.

Google News Alert (http://news.google.com/): Just because we are talking the latest technology and cutting-edge web data mining there is no need to forget the obvious. Google's News Alert service is a great way to set up 'trip wires' intended to alert you when certain trends begin to break. In order to set it up you need to navigate to the Google News Alert page and click on the Google News Alert link: (http://www.google.com/alerts?hl=en). Next, you define a topic, by setting any number of keywords and phrases that retrieved items need to have, the type of news you want, how often you want it, and your email. That's it, there is nothing more to do. You'll have to confirm your email, but I've created Google news alerts in about 45 seconds, tops. Once your account is verified, you have access not only to Google's news tracker, but a ton of other cool stuff; including Google Groups, Answers, and Web APIs. Go ahead and sign in and further personalize your news tracking. The online interface and instructions make this process easy. Google will now send you news alerts that you have chosen to your email inbox, at the rate you want, from once a day, once a week, or as the news happens. Google has access to literally thousands of news sources, and I've found that when I need more of a variety of sources on one subject, they manage to deliver.

Real Time Picture Search (http://picfog.com): If you are looking for a trend which truly is big enough, or need information on something which is becoming hot across the web the chances are that there is a lot of pictorial material associated with it. Picfog is a real-time web search engine which indexes the latest pics to appear across social networks and can throw up some surprising results.

Search Torrent sites (http://www.youtorrent.com/): Torrent sites are file download sites. Activity in them is a good indication of popular interests, trends and what's peeking across a large segment of the online population. YouTorrent is a real-time search engine which looks at what is happening across different Torrent sites. Useful as a point of additional, purely corroborative research but not as the main means of getting real-time information which will be used for long-term business marketing planning.

The real-time web search tools detailed here have the ability to give you corporate-style quality information for a little investment of your time. If you are doping searches and your marketing plans depend on them you will need to give yourself two – three weeks and record the results you find so that you can then compare them.

The real-time web, of course, is a tool, just like any other and its effectiveness does not come just from using it (you could argue that part is easy) but from knowing just when to use it.

Chapter #4

How to decide when to use the real time web

Five years ago, we thought of the Web as a new medium, not a new economy.
Clement Mok

The real-time web takes the internet to the next level. Since its inception, first as a medium and then as a place to do business, we have seen one trend which has held true: it has gone, increasingly, towards greater immediacy and more interactivity for the end user.

The web has graduated, steadily and unremittingly, from the place where you would find the corporate brochure set up as a website to the one medium where you can turn to for cheaper services, better information and real-time interaction.

The journey from where it started to here has not been an easy one and the road is littered with the carcasses of failed technologies, failed concepts and failed business models. Yet along that way we have gained the ability to increasingly get, online, the immediacy of going into a real-world store and asking an expert shop assistant for information and help before we make a purchase.

It is this which makes the real-time web so exciting, challenging, addictive and so full of opportunity. And it is this defining need to connect which will also determine, for us, as users when and how to make use of it.

Mastering the real-time web

Whenever we do anything, anywhere, we are trading off time (and effort) for gain. If we take the business-like view that both time and effort cost (in the sense that if you invested each into something which is immediately profitable you would be making money as a result) then anything which we do online (or offline for that matter) is an investment which needs to return a pay-off.

Right now I will say that by far the most common mistake you can make is to jump on a bandwagon without understanding why. You are reading this book so I will assume you are exploring possibilities which will help you turn the opportunities afforded by the real-time web to your advantage. In order for you to be true to your intention you also need to discipline yourself in the way you use the web.

Technology is addictive and the real-time web with its promise of immediate interaction and a quick trade-off of time and response is one of the most addictive trends at the moment. Using it can become as meaningless, time-consuming and self-defeating as sharpening pencils and tidying up desks and filing letters used to be in the real world when we did not want to engage in real work.

So promise yourself that the moment you see that the real-time web simply has no impact on how you currently work or what you do, move away from it and focus on what really works for you. The reason I mention this now, here, is that I have, far too often, found myself consulting in companies where their ideas flow, online research and general sense of excitement about the development of the online world far exceeds the application this has on their day to day work.

A company like that is an exciting place to be in, in terms that it is caught in a stage of perpetual transition where it redefines itself and what it does but the cost of that is productivity and profitability. Companies which are in this state face two stark choices: move quickly to the next phase where this excitement is translated into actionable projects which are focused on contributing to the bottom line or close down.

The real-time web, at the moment, gives us two possible uses which promise to deliver value in return for the investment in time and effort we are being asked to make: research and marketing. Both, when handled properly, are invaluable in their effect and their effectiveness, so let's go and see each in turn.

Using the real-time web for research

Whatever type of business you might be in, in this world, I can guarantee that someone else is already doing it. If you're the kind of person who is content to simply 'dog' competitors, nipping at their heels and trying to steal from their plate knowing what they do (and how) is necessary.

Research in the real-time web using Twitter is something used by business people, business angels, investors, journalists and business owners checking out the trends and the actions of their competition.

If you're the kind of person who tries to steal a march on the competition by introducing something which differentiates you from them then you need to not just know what your competitors are doing and how but also understand why they are doing it. Research in the real-time web then becomes, for you, crucial.

Either way you need to be able to do the following: Research the real-time web and understand what to make of the results you find. In the following section we shall see how each of these can be achieved.

Discovering trends and ideas

With entrepreneurs and journalists data-mining Twitter every single day for information we begin to realize that the immediacy provided by the micro-blogging site has actually managed to significantly shorten the loop between information first becoming available and then being found in a place where those who need to use it can actually find it.

Twitter's success means that every second of the day its users post hundreds of thousands of tidbits of information which, if used properly, can deliver insights which can lead to new ideas, better marketing and a more closely coordinated relationship between companies and their clients.

In order to use Twitter properly it is important that we understand just how it works.

Know How to Use Twitter

Fortunately, using Twitter to broadcast messages is easy. There is not much convention to remember as it works much like an online SMS service. Basically, after you have created an account there, you can just type in and send.

The difference is, to get the most out of Twitter, you need to know a few conventions regarding its syntax:

- **@username – Reply.** Tweets that start with an @ and then a username is a reply to that user. If you follow someone and want to reply to them, using reply is the way to go.
- **#tag – Hashtag.** Hash that is immediately followed by a tag (called hashtag) in Twitter is a community-driven convention for adding additional context and metadata to your tweets. The contexts could be events, disasters, memes, or others.

Two Main Ways to Perform Research with Twitter

Twitterrers with a lot of followers certainly have an edge here. If you have a group of people who are willing to hear what you have to say, or if you have friends whose professional opinion you value and who you can call anytime, you can just do that and ask them for opinions or anything.

This leads us to the first way to perform research with Twitter, which is to…

1. **Ask.** If you follow someone, for instance, you will occasionally find them asking questions. Not only does that encourage participation from their followers, but they also get the information they need to write their next blog post, or just as an insight to understand their

audience better. What you could ask the followers is limited only by your imagination. Questions that can be answered quickly are winners. With the right engagement, results will pour in soon after you tweet. Directing the followers to a series of questions, such as a survey, on the Web may work but you need to be aware of the time factor. People who spend time online work against the clock. They only have so much of it to spend and asking them to spend time answering questions for surveys which will benefit you is often counterproductive. So it is always best to keep things simple in terms of a single question which anyone can spend a microsecond (or two) answering. If you think you need help in putting together better questions in Twitter, check out the Appendix at the end of this book with a set of practical, useful guidelines.

2. **Search.** By using publicly accessible data, you can also learn a lot. For instance, if I search for tweets from a particular person and his followers, I'd be able to find out answers from their questions and use those for writing ideas or even books. In one particular case a set of questions and answers on a specific SEO topic suddenly made me aware of how there was a gap in the market in terms of the information available and this led, directly to a new book on practical SEO steps, called

'SEO Help' which became an Amazon best-seller on three continents.

Twitter is a valuable real-time knowledge resource and knowing which tools to use, when is exactly what it is about.

Here are some essential Twitter tools you should know about

With these tools under your belt, you should be able to get started in using Twitter's data effectively and be able to find out information breaking in real-time when you most need it.

- **Twitter client** – www.twhirl.org. This is a handy application which allows you to do two things at once, First you can use it to post updates to Twitter directly. Second, you can use it to carry out search inside Twitter itself employing either Twitter Search (http://search.twitter.com/) and Tweet Scan (http://tweetscan.com/) each of which will give you results depending on how deeply their respective algorithm has indexed Twitter.
- **General search.** Both Twitter Search and TweetScan provide reliable search for Twitter's data, but the former allows you to drill down your search queries using the Advanced search feature which is handy when you are chasing a query which requires more information than you would easily find.

- **Tag search.** Twitter Search is also able to search for tags, but #hashtags returns a graphical representation of the trend for a specific tag. This is an important feature in quickly deciding just how important something is or not.
- **Conversation search.** If you want to search for previous conversations, again Twitter Search is able to provide you with the information. If there is a conversation related to a tweet, you will see a link to **Show Conversation**.
- **Location search – Twitter Local** (http://twitterlocal.net/) is great when you want to carry out research on a local business and its reputation as well as find out about their activities.
- **Keyword search - Monitter** (http://www.monitter.com/) lets you monitor three keywords live at the same time with the ability to nail down geographic area. This is a great feature to use when you are tracking a localized event and are looking for information or want to follow a trend about something breaking in an area now.
- **Topical research.** Twitter is nothing if not an ingenious way to find out information about real-time activities. If you are tracking a company or even a person and they are active in Twitter then by using Tweet Stats (http://tweetstats.com) you will get a graphic-driven, very detailed representation of their

activities, what they are doing, when, in what frequency and through which interfaces.

- **Trending URL search.** Twitter URL (www.twitterurly.com) is a service which tracks and serves results on the URLs submitted by Twitter users. This is a feature which useful in unearthing trends just before they break and in taking the pulse of the popular vote (so to speak) when it comes to breaking events. It will also help you to assess just what impact a particular story or event you are tracking is likely to have by seeing if it is trending or not.

Using Twitter for brand and company news marketing

Because of its immediate nature Twitter is also ideal for what we call opportunistic brand marketing.

1. **Engage your CEO (if you're in a large company, or yourself if you're not) in social media.** The communication revolution of our times means that the use of social media is the primary means to get the word out about your brand rather than an additional extra which is nice to have. While it is great to write long blog posts about the things which really motivate your company in its niche the reality is that there is little time to actually consistently devote to such an

activity. In addition the very pressure of work itself makes it unlikely that the discipline required in order to maintain a long-term, meaningful informational campaign will is ever going to be found. This is where Twitter is simply a life saver. It is off-the-cuff, short and yet accessible enough in terms of reach to actually have an impact. Anyone who is at the heart of a brand or a company, usually, has something interesting to say. Twitter allows you to say it fast, casually, with a minimum of effort and maximum impact. What's more, because you can send it from almost anywhere, it becomes less of a bind to stick to it and more likely that it will become a news stream which generates the charm, stickiness and quirkiness which social marketing needs in order to succeed these days.

2. **Keep in touch with the media.** Today no company which wants to make it online can afford to not have a social media presence. This means that beyond creating content you also need to be aware of what is going on in the online media world. Again, Twitter is your best bet. Many media stars, bloggers and reporters Tweet about their work and passions and by following them you usually get at least a few of them following you. Beyond the value of using this way to connect with those who may give you online exposure there is also the additional bonus of understanding what is trending now and why.

Page 59

3. **Monitor what's being said about you.** These days you cannot afford to be blind, deaf and dumb about what's being said about you online. This should be part of your company's monitoring policy regarding its brand name anyway but by checking you also make it possible to find allies where you least look for them. A positive mention by someone you do not know may lead to fresh opportunities or new, unlooked for, deals, all of which help widen the impact of your brand. Twitter is a powerful tool with great mobility (you can get Tweet alerts on your phone) and its clever use will allow you to maintain a high-visibility, low-cost presence with great reach and immediacy (just like my favorite bakery which we saw at the beginning of this book).

4. **Announce specials, deals or sales.** Twitter is everything Newsletters promised to be and failed to live up to. It is direct, up-to-the-minute and immediate. If you are in any kind of business which operates locally as well as globally (through your website) the use of Twitter to announce special deals, special offers and even time-limited competitions. If you are a retailer or anyone who often has special offers, you can use Twitter to announce these deals instantly to a large audience. This means that you have the ability to use the web to attract local traffic

and better manage your trade and market your merchandise globally.

5. **Live updates, product demonstrations, events or conferences.** Twitter is a great last minute marketing tool. It bridges the gap between traditional advertising with its long lead times and the instant marketing a billboard announcement gives you. Because Twitter appears where your potential customers are it has the ability to produce surprising results: A tweet saying "David Amerland book signing at John Lewis Oxford Street, London, now" for instance drew 900 local customers in the space of an hour and a half, something which would not have been achieved in any other way.

6. **Promote blog articles, webinars, interesting news and more.** Twitter is at its best when it acts as a hub, cross-linking many other different posts. Use it to announce company news, blog posts, events, press releases which appear elsewhere and you will find that it is capable of driving traffic to your main websites almost effortlessly. During the writing of this book, for instance, Twitter became my release valve. Every hour, on the hour I posted a message about *SEO Help*, my book on practical search engine optimization and how it could help the new webmaster remove the uncertainty form their online marketing. This amounted to between five and six messages a day for about four

months. The result was that *SEO Help* which had been languishing around the middle of the Amazon.com top 100, shot to the top reaching position 7 within a week and then rarely fell below the top 25 best-selling books, all because of 'a few tweets'.

Twitter, of course, is only one aspect, albeit a vital one, of the real-time web. The site which started it all, made Twitter popular and got Google thinking about the real-time web is none other than Facebook, the world's largest online community site.

Chapter #5

Understanding the strengths and weaknesses of Facebook

For most of the '90s and the first part of this decade, content providers who wanted to publish online only needed to worry about the graphical web browser.
Mike Davidson

Facebook is, now, so large, so well-known and so powerful that it would have made sense to start talking about the real-time web with it, rather than wait until Chapter five to discuss it. There are some really good reasons why I didn't cover it earlier. Facebook is part of the real-time web on the basis of its Wall posting functionality. At the time of writing this book it is still undergoing development which is unclear in which direction it will push it. Should it become a truly 'walled garden' on the web it will continue to be an integral part of your real-time marketing but it will need to be handled differently to the rest of your online marketing tools.

For now however, everything we will cover here is valid and Facebook is an active part of the real-time web.

Why do you need a Facebook page?

There has to be a reason for everything. Facebook marketing is no exception. In order to justify the time and effort required to use Facebook properly we really need to understand what it gives us.

At the time of writing Facebook is some 500 million users strong. It has become a global social network the likes of which we have not seen before and it is trying to create a walled garden variety internet where everything that matters happens within the Facebook universe.

To that end it has created indexing barriers with Google allowing the search engine to penetrate only within the few superficial layers of Facebook and it has been working on its own eCommerce and advertising systems.

Whatever the success of these will ultimately be, what matters now is that Facebook has become the world's stickiest site with many online users spending much of their online available time there.

There is a little more to it than that. Seeing how 2010 became the year when Facebook delivered more data than Google and it became one of the principle means of discovering and sharing news and also seeing how the Facebook 'Share' button is ubiquitous on the web; allowing Facebookers to practically take their off-Facebook activities back with them, a powerful presence in Facebook is now a vital aspect of every online marketing plan worthy of the name.

There is more. Because Facebook is one of the many elements checked by a search engine, a presence there confers additional value to your website's SEO status. Plus, it also helps to deliver traffic to you and help more of your target audience find you.

The final benefit of Facebook is that it has made viral marketing easier and its presence and development has speeded up the inception of the real-time web.

What do you need to have on Facebook?

Now that we have seen the benefits of Facebook the question has to be what do you exactly need to have in order to 'get there'.

Ok, here is the list and the pitfalls to be aware of:

1. You need to create a Facebook profile. Since you will be using this for business do not fall into the trap of making it the kind of profile that will show pictures of you at a stag party and holiday snapshots of you in Bangkok or at your favourite spa enjoying a relaxing massage (I have seen all of this in client Facebook profiles). If you want to have a personal page on Facebook (or if you already have one) go to the Privacy Settings and make sure its contents are visible only to those who are really your friends. If this will not work, for the purpose of marketing your business it may be worth it if you create a second Facebook profile (yes, I know it's against Facebook rules but this is a small infringement you may have to make) and start fresh, there, with greater openness so you can socially network. If you need help in creating a Facebook profile page or if you already have one and you are not sure it is right for your business needs

check with **Appendix 2** at the back of this book.

2. You need to create a Facebook Page. Unlike Facebook profiles which have stringent rules in terms of who you add and how, Facebook Pages are promotional pages created to promote, on Facebook, individuals, businesses or products. Those who join a Facebook page by clicking on the 'Like' button become fans of the page and you, as the page owner, can message them each week. This becomes a powerful means of providing additional marketing with the potential for it to go viral. Facebook pages have been optimized by Facebook to do several things which help their promotion. They are, for instance, linked to the news stream of their fans for real-time updates. So the instant you put something on your Facebook Page Wall, all those who are fans of that page will see it updated on their news stream and those who are their friends will see their interaction with your page on their news stream. This way you get promoted with relatively little more effort than you would put in the updating of a regular Facebook page. The second thing, which is also important, is that

Facebook Pages have no limits to the number of Fans. While Facebook profiles have a limit of 5,000 Facebook pages can have, potentially, an unlimited number of fans. Fans who 'Like' a Facebook Page (and therefore become part of its membership) can be actively marketed to through regular updates. One word of caution is needed here. When you do send updates to Fans you will need to make sure that they are cleverly written and very targeted. Anything too generic will most likely be reported to Facebook as spam by those receiving it even though they are already fans of a page. There are many reasons why this may happen. Sometimes people forget that they are fans of a page and when they do receive a message they regard is as being unsolicited, as they get a lot of messages from Facebook groups, pages and applications it becomes difficult for them to keep track of. Some others may simply be annoyed by Facebook in general and others still simply mark anything they receive as spam. The fact is that a small percentage of people will report a Facebook Page's update as spam. Facebook has a completely automated process in place which kicks in the moment they receive some unspecified to us number of spam reports. The process can include an automatic ban of a page irrespective of the number of fans it may have and the deletion of a person's profile. While this may sound totally arbitrary and undemocratic it is, at present, within the guidelines of operation Facebook has in place so it is important to bear this in mind and make sure that your messages to the fans of your Facebook Page are within those frequency and tone boundaries which would make it difficult for anyone to mark as spam.

In order to market on Facebook you need, of course, first to be there which is what the preceding section has been all about. There are pros and cons of being on Facebook. Because Facebook is a vital element of online marketing and SEO these days there is no question that you need to have a presence there. So, before we even get to the pros and cons let's go and look at how Facebook can be used for marketing purposes.

How to market on Facebook

If you are going to be effective in your Facebook marketing you need to be able to minimise the time and effort required to do it well and for that you really need to have a blueprint of sorts which will enable you to be consistent in your Facebook messages and also take the hard work out of having to think each time just what kind of message you should put there.

Like any guide the blueprint you create for yourself has a certain amount of tolerance. It is next to impossible to get it just right every time and the appeal and success of your Facebook marketing messages will also depend upon the time of the day you post them and the changing demographics of your audience.

The guide which follows will help you in creating the Facebook marketing blueprint you need and its ten steps are intended to make life easier for you:

1. Be unique - There's nothing worse than a bland Facebook page. Research has shown that Facebook users divide their attention on more than 60 different things when they are on Facebook. Compared to the traditional way of marketing online where we were used to a website visitor coming to a website and then having, for the few microseconds which we had to capture their attention, a monopoly upon them, Facebook is more like trying to catch the attention of speeding traffic with a billboard, with one exception. If their attention is engaged the billboard travels with them throughout their online journey. This means that if your page is exactly like any other page your 'billboard' stands a good chance of simply being lost in the crowd. So it is important to start your Facebook page with all those elements which signify memorability and think hard how you will work to engage your Facebook audience's attention. Consider that what works best on Facebook (as it does in most online situations) is something which is clever, fun, ads value, solves a problem users may have or provides an additional resource. Provided you can do this on your Facebook page you will get people who join, promote it to their friends and keep coming back to check.

2. Don't use a generic landing page – The Facebook Page most people who are on Facebook are familiar with is the Wall. This is where you tend to interact with those who visit your page and this is where they leave messages and comments and you get to respond to them. In terms of engaging your audience this is a great page to interact. It keeps things low-key and yet generates a high level of persistence and can be very addictive. All the things which make the Wall a winner, however, work against you when it comes to first time visitors. There are many factors for this.

First of all the Wall is messy and not always your best work. Imagine, you are busy responding to a lengthy string of messages where an in-joke is beginning to develop. Great for those who stick with the page and whose comments generate more interest and publicise it to their own circle of friends, really bad form for the first time visitor who thinks he stumbled onto amateur hour, or worse. Second, the comment/response 'game' upon which the Wall's interaction is based can become off-putting to someone new who may suddenly feel that your Facebook Page is a kind of closed shop for those in the know. Thirdly, the Wall does not allow you to properly promote your Page to attract new recruits as it is seen by those who are already fans of your Page and do not really want to feel they are constantly being marketed to. Facebook allows you to customize your Page in many ways and it is up to you to find a way to make it unique. The landing page you present to those who find your Facebook Page for the first time really needs to be different from any other landing page and also work a little like a website in terms of the message it delivers to those who see it for the first time. In other words it really needs to tell them what your page does, who you are and what is in it for them if they join you.

3. Give something away quickly – This follows on from the previous step. Facebook is all about engagement and engagement is like BO not even your best friends will tell you if you are not achieving it but you will see if you are by the number of fans your page gets. In order to create that instant engagement factor with people who first see your page consider giving away something which truly offers value and allows them to understand that you are about a two-way engagement rather than old-fashioned, one-way marketing. This will not just help increase conversions to your page from visitors to fans but it will also allow them to publicise and share your page with their friends.

4. Use a large profile picture – It's true what they say about the web. People look at pictures first and text a poor second. Facebook has become the largest photograph sharing site in the planet exactly because of that. Make sure that you have a large picture on your profile, with something clever enough to help stop the eye, long enough for everything else there to engage the mind.

5. Tag fans in photos – The tag feature in photographs is one of the most controversial ones. It is very easy to apply and incredibly easy to overuse which means that it can quickly become annoying and that just kills its effectiveness. Like most abilities Facebook gives you which are intended to be used for social purposes and are, instead, utilized to aid the promotion of business, this also needs to be used with a certain degree of restraint and always within a broader online Facebook marketing plan.

The thing to remember with tagging is that people tagged in photographs are automatically notified by Facebook alerts which make them log on and visit your Page in order to actually see the photographs in which they have been tagged. If you have an offline business and you could, for example, photograph your customers and they are on Facebook (and statistically this is likely) you suddenly have gained a powerful means of getting them to interact with you online and be marketed to in a subtle, contextually social way.

Page73

Your fans also have the ability to upload photos as well. (This might require some moderation on your part. As with anything user generated, you might get some spam, etc.) Allowing fans to upload and tag themselves and friends in your pages automatically adds a nice social "hook" to your page.

6. Use contests - Contests are a great way to make your fan page more engaging, and they also give incentive for potential fans to join. Contests that include giveaways can be excellent marketing tools if they're done properly. Again do remember that this is a social network. Make your giveaway fun, with value and engaging in nature and you are onto a winner.

7. Integrate multiple social networks – Time is always against you. Given the need to work with Twitter and Facebook (these two are imperative) and MySpace, YouTube and Flickr it is a given that you will not have sufficient time each day, every week to make it happen. Luckily, already, there are on Facebook a number of applications which allow you to integrate Twitter and MySpace with Facebook so that a post in one appears in all the other ones saving you a lot of time and providing a truly integrated approach to your social marketing.

8. Thank people for becoming your fans - Remember that we live in the age of permission marketing. When people become Fans of your Page they give you permission to market to them. This means that you can never just take them for granted.

You need to acknowledge them in some way, certainly find ways to thank them, sometimes even just saying 'Thank You'. This small gesture can be huge in spreading goodwill about your Page and brand. It might even give users more incentive to share your contests and resources on your fan page.

9. Don't treat your fans like kids – Here is where you need to show your ingenuity and your grasp of what you are trying to do with your online marketing. A Facebook Page always brings you more than just who you think in terms of visitors. Although you will inevitably have a specific customer profile which you will use, in the first instant, to kick-start your marketing the chances are that you will soon find out who your real audience are. It is hugely important that you fine-tune your marketing messages to take all this into account. Get it wrong, over-react, be too serious or not serious enough, be condescending or too curt and you will begin to lose fans and tarnish your online reputation.

10. Keep at it – Be engaged yourself. If you fail to take your Facebook Page seriously, actively make daily updates to it and create the kind of comment, counter-comment, fun posts and fun atmosphere it will die. The thing is that you will have to start off with content and maintain it even in the initial stages of the Page when the fans are few and interaction almost non-existent. It is usually at this stage which, depending on your Page, can last anywhere from a few weeks to a few months that most Facebook Page owners give up, wondering why Facebook marketing did not work for them. The truth is that had they given it sufficient time it would have, so really do keep at it.

0100100101100110001000000111100101101111011
1010101110010001000000110111101101110011011
0001101001011011100110010100100000011011010
1100001011001001101011011001010111010001110
1001011011001100111001000000110110101100101
1011100110111001101100001011001110110010101
1100110010000001100100011011110010000001101
1100110111101110100000100000011001010111000
0110001101101001011101000110010100100000011
1100101101111011101010010000011001100110010
0101110010011100110111011010000101100001000000
1110100011010000110010101111001001000000110
0001011100100110010100100000011101010110111
0011011000110100101101011011001010110110001
1110010010000001110100011011110010000001110
1110110111101110010011010101100100000011011
0110111000100000011110010110111101101010011
1001000100000011000110111101010111001101111101
0001101111011011010110010101110010011100110
0101110

Chapter #6

What else is there?

Advances in computer technology and the Internet have changed the way America works, learns, and communicates. The Internet has become an integral part of America's economic, political, and social life. **Mike Bill Clinton**

This is a practical book, written to help you put into effect practical steps which will enable you to make your online business successful. For the past sixteen years I have lived in the web, chronicled its development and lived through the cycles of its patterns. There is a fascination this kind of lifestyle and work engenders which verges on the addictive and is, often, an end in itself.

Sadly however it has no place in this book. Apart from the web itself and the dynamics which govern it I have another passion which runs almost as deep and it is the unshakeable belief that the web is the kind of paradigm shift we have all been waiting for. It is the great equalizer which levels the playing field and can help those who have no huge organization behind them or even deep pockets to stand up to and beat corporations at their own game.

This David and Goliath scenario is beneficent to us all. By providing competition at a level which most Corporations would like to ignore it forces them to become more competitive, more adaptive, more engaging and more humane. The web, as its real-time marketing trend suggests, is heading towards personalization. It is making the global, local with every meaning of the metaphor.

So this book is about tools. You have seen the two major components of the real-time web: Twitter and Facebook. You have also seen how to use them, when and why. You understand now that social marketing is an activity which is not complex and which does not require anything more than a little persistence, a well worked-out gameplan and the ability to work hard when it comes to implementing it. All of which really do bring us to the title of this chapter. If you use Twitter and Facebook, what else is there and how should you use it? Well, this, the final chapter of this book tells you exactly what else you

can use and how to use it in order to maximise the
impact of your real-time marketing on the web and
save valuable time while doing so.

Other social network tools you need to be aware of

Tumblr (www.tumblr.com) is a mix between Twitter
and Facebook. It allows you to use it as an extended
content and Blog posting network and also as a
microblogging site.

Tumblr has the added attraction that it can be
linked to from Twitter (which itself can be linked to
Facebook) so that it becomes part of your real-time
web marketing. This way a post made on Facebook
the Wall, appears in Twitter and appears in Tumblr.
Apart from the fact that this one post triples the
exposure it would otherwise get, it also creates an
online momentum which really helps when it comes
to the importance search engines give to your content.

Signing up to Tumblr is pretty straightforward,
simply go to the website and register an account.
When it comes to the name of the page you choose
there it will help if you use your business name or the
name of your website you are trying to promote,
something along the lines of:
www.mygreatbusinessidea.tumblr.com. This way
you are getting an additional feed in the search engine
index which is great for your SEO.

FriendFeed (www.friendfeed.com) is the first
"social network integrator" I encountered. It can
aggregate feeds from Facebook and Twitter which

means that it also aggregates feeds posted to Tumblr and MySpace. MySpace deserves a section all of its own and we will deal with it a little later in the chapter, so for now let's look at one more vital real-time web component: social commenting.

Social commenting as marketing

The Facebook Wall and its ability to spark off discussion threads where people add comments (sometimes gibberish and sometimes serious and always useful) has an addictive quality which many commenting systems have sought to emulate. None has come closer to it than Disqus.

Disqus is an online service that offers a centralized discussion platform for websites. It was founded in May 2007. It supports integration with Gravatar (http://en.gravatar.com), Facebook, Twitter, and other social networks. As of June 10, 2008, the service had over 150 thousand registered users and 17 thousand communities, which included blogs and websites. As of August 10, 2010, the service had over 13 million registered users and 500 thousand communities.

The idea of Disqus is that as social commentary you take your comments with you (much like the Facebook 'Like' button allows you to take Facebook with you). When a user visits one of the websites using Disqus and posts a comment, for instance, the comment is submitted to Disqus and saved on the user's profile (provided he has one). If the user does have a Disqus account, then it tracks all their comments across all the websites that use Disqus as a comment system.

This often leads to greater exposure, better user generated content, and the ability to generate viral marketing. Like most things which happen in the real-time web, Disqus can provide exposure to your online business within a social framework and at a relatively low cost, provided you succeed in engaging users.

Making space at MySpace

MySpace (www.myspace.com) used to be the primary online network in the world. If we take the clock back as recently as three years ago MySpace was still the place where everything happened. Today it is a secondary, though still important element of the real-time web. Let's go and see, briefly, why it fell out of favor (trust me, it's important) and how you should use it today.

First things first. MySpace fell out of favor for the same reason Facebook managed to overtake it: ease of use, clarity of programming and design and the kind of critical mass which allows you to take the social as well as the business side of your life online.

Although at the tail end of 2010 MySpace underwent a massive redesign which now allows it to look slicker and more navigable, the fact that it still does not have the immediacy of response you get on Facebook and the freedom it gives you in customizing your page there tends to produce pages which still take a long time to load and, more often than not, lack any clarity as to their purpose. Unlike Facebook,

MySpace never felt the need to separate personal profiles from business with the result that there is a clouding of each page to the point of ineffectiveness.

Despite these drawbacks MySpace is a major online presence. It has a large number of devoted users and it gets indexed by Google which counts in terms of SEO for a website. So discount it we won't, which brings us to the question: how should it be best used in order to provide results in terms of online visibility and viral marketing potential for a website?

Certainly the evidence suggests that provided you can crack the formula MySpace can help you generate a strong following. A classic example of this success is internet star Tila Tequila (http://www.myspace.com/tilatequila) who, before she had a breakdown and lost the plot, managed to leverage a MySpace network of friends numbering just over 1 million to make a decent living in advertising and merchandise.

The first step of using MySpace for marketing is to have a profile there which means you really need to go to www.myspace.com register a profile and put in your website address, some pictures and a description of what your online business does, in order to properly flesh out your profile.

Once you have done that and established a presence the next step should be developing a marketing plan. The steps below tell you just how MySpace can be best utilized for that:

Step 1: Run ads in the classified section. This is the most obvious way to market using MySpace.com.

Step 2: Put up posts in the forum. There are forums that you can post in and add your affiliate links in the signatures.

Step 3: Create a profile just for marketing. In other words don't use your regular MySpace account. Build relationships and start marketing. Make sure to put up some information, pictures and interests which are relevant to what you do. People will buy things from people who they like, so it can't be just all about the marketing. When you put up your profile make sure to put up info about your company or products.

Step 4: Tell people about products you are interested in or your product on your "What are You Doing Right Now" section. You can also add a link here which can be clicked to take those who see it to your website. Again make sure not to spam people too often with this.

Step 5: Add friends with like interests. You can add friends with similar interests by joining groups. So if you have a dog product to market join a group about pets or dogs, and add friends from that group. If you have a website about scuba diving then join a group related to diving. You can also use a friend adder (go to: http://uberadd.com/ or http://www.adderdemon.com/), which is a piece of software that will expedite and automate the process of finding and adding friends.

The fact is that whatever happens on the web there will always be space for MySpace and there should always be space for it in your online marketing strategy.

010011010110000101101011011001010010000011
110010110111101110101011100100010000001101 1
110110111001101100011010010110111001100101 0
010000001101101011000010111001001101011011 0
010101110100011010010110111001100111001000 0
001110111011011111011100100110101100100000 01
100110011011110111001000100000011110010110 1
111011101010010000000110010101110110011001 01
011100100111100100100000011101000110100101 1
0110101100101001011100

Chapter #7
Going viral

Marketing is too important to be left to the marketing department. **David Packard**

This is the one chapter in the book where the title is misleading. Going viral, on the web is when something is picked up by individual web users and promoted independently and the potential to go viral exists with almost everything you do in the real-time web. So this is not really so much a chapter about going viral (this depends on your ability to post content which is compelling and shareable) as it is about looking at a media channel on the web which sits astride traditional web and the real-time web but which features heavily in many successful viral campaigns: video.

There are many video sharing channels on the web: Google Video (http://video.google.com/), Vimeo (http://vimeo.com/), Hulu (http://vimeo.com/), Metacafe (http://www.metacafe.com), Flickr (www.flickr.com) and Photobucket (www.photobucket.com) to mention but a few. A Google search with the search term 'free video sharing site' will give you hundreds of others. Video has been the success story of the web. Better processors, faster web connections and improved browsers have made it possible to share and watch video online in a thoroughly seamless experience.

As a result of the ability to share video and the relative ease within which many web videos can be shared has led to a mini-revolution on the web which has allowed adverts, promotions and even company news to be spread at the click of a button.

When it comes to web video standing head and shoulders above all others is a Google property: YouTube (www.youtube.com). YouTube has become so popular on the web that you have an hour of video content uploaded on it every second of the day. This means that over 10 hours of viewing time was uploaded to it in the time it took you to read this paragraph.

YouTube's power is such that it has become a vital aspect of any online visibility campaign. It has become the main means of viral campaigns and it has often played exactly the David and Goliath scenario which has allowed a small operator or even an individual to take on and beat the marketing behemoths.

When it comes to the power of YouTube there are a few stories on the web which stand out from the rest because they combined a certain humor or fun approach in addition to a serious message. This combination of fun with something a little more serious is what makes a web video campaign more likely to go viral as successful videos, like successful blockbuster films contain something for almost everyone of those who see them.

The power of YouTube to inverse the traditional balance of power between the individual and the Corporation is such that not factoring it into your online marketing is to create a blind spot which can stop your online business from growing.

The best way to see how YouTube can be used is to actually look at some examples, which is what we will do now.

United Airlines Breaks Guitars

When it comes to air travel the worst nightmare of anyone is that they will have their luggage either lost or damaged as a result of airline mishandling and then face the tedious task of having to struggle with the airline for some compensation.

In 2008 a relatively successful but little known singer/songwriter by the name of Dave Carroll was busy travelling in the US with members of his band,

Sons of Maxwell, using the airline giant, United Airlines, to get to a gig in Nebraska.

He had a Taylor Guitar which he checked into luggage and happened to witness being handled a little more roughly than it should by the luggage handling staff. What happened next is now an internet legend.

He discovered later that the $3500 guitar was severely damaged. United Airlines didn't deny the incident occurred but for nine months the various people Dave communicated with were reluctant to take responsibility for dealing with the damage. Finally said they would do nothing to compensate him for the loss.

Finally fed up with So he promised the last person to finally say "no" - a Ms. Irlweg - that he would write and produce three songs about the experience with United Airlines and make videos for each to be viewed online by anyone in the world.

In 2009 the video went live on YouTube. In just ten days the video registered four million hits on YouTube and generated a massive viral wave on the web. It wiped out $180 million from United Airlines stock and shares as they dropped 10pc virtually overnight and they forced the airline giant to acknowledge their mistake, make good on the damage caused and promise to reform the way they handled complaints.

The Dave Caroll videos became a most-shared and talked about term on Twitter and countless bloggers, websites and even books (like mine) mentioned it as a classic example of what can be achieved with a little ingenuity, some passion and real heart on the web.

If you want to see Dave Carroll's website where he mentions the videos you can do so here: http://www.davecarrollmusic.com/ubg/.

The three videos on YouTube can be seen at:
1. http://www.davecarrollmusic.com/ubg/song1/
2. http://www.davecarrollmusic.com/ubg/song2/
3. http://www.davecarrollmusic.com/ubg/song3/

They can also be searched for independently on the YouTube site where the first video released currently has almost 10 million hits: http://www.youtube.com/watch?v=5YGc4zOqozo

The example is notable because Dave Carroll can actually sing and was able to infuse quality and humor in a situation which struck a chord with many viewers which then enabled the video to go viral.

I know that not everyone can sing or play the guitar or even have access to the talented people who generously donated their time, knowledge and energy which went into the making of each of Dave Carroll's videos.

That, however, is exactly the point and why I mention the videos here. Dave Carroll's videos display all the requirements of a successful viral video campaign. His kind of happened. By understanding what made his work you can then make sure the next viral video success is one you have planned.

Before we go and see the ingredients however let's look at how the success of Dave Carroll's videos helped him and those who were smart enough to respond and how they hurt United Airlines who took the Corporate approach of faceless unaccountability.

Using Video to get your point across

Dave Carroll had a real grievance with United Airlines and, prior to making the videos, he head genuinely exhausted every means at his disposal in getting a resolution.

The success of his videos helped him and his band as a brand in getting better known for their music. It also helped in the propagation of his own personal brand, a privilege which he was careful not to abuse as a more direct video he made after the success of his first video about United Airlines shows: http://www.youtube.com/watch?v=5YGc4zOqozo.

The noise surrounding Dave Carroll's videos and their popularity across the web did not go unnoticed by the company which makes the guitars Dave Carroll uses who, very cleverly, also responded with a video: http://www.youtube.com/watch?v=n12WFZq2_0.

Their video response drew over half a million views and made the brand better known across the web (and the world). It most certainly helped their business and certainly helped in the recognition of their brand by personalizing it.

While Dave Carroll's videos are pretty slick productions the most successful videos on the web, these days are relatively low-key affairs. Dave Carroll was not marketing, he was complaining. If you market to the online video viewing community you should steer clear from anything overtly slick and go for something which is simple, direct and as honest as possible.

Here are the elements you need in order to help make your video successful:

1. Make the subject of your video about something real. It is ok to market provided you tackle a real problem your potential clients have and provide a real solution.

2. Make it honest. Forget the marketing gimmicks and slickness of advertising. These are all so last century. In the 21st century honesty and sincerity are the tools which help you win. If your solution or product really works then say so and simply explain why.

3. Make it logical. Advertising is all about emotional responses. It creates a need rather than provide a solution. Your video should give facts, figures and explain logically why what you suggest people access or buy is really a great solution for them, using English anyone should be able to understand.

4. Do not make it too long. It's true that attention spans are shortening and, on the web, they are shorter than ever. Dave Carroll's videos are long because of the music and the visual storyline he has incorporated into them. Chances are

you will not have the means to do the same, so try and keep them to a maximum of two minutes and, preferably, as short as thirty seconds.

5. Make it entertaining. This is the hardest thing to do. As the Tony Robbins quote in Chapter 3 so aptly states we really are in an entertainment rather than an information age. You may have found the cure to Cancer, unless you can also, somehow, make it entertaining, it is unlikely it will go viral. So here is something which will require a lot of thought and quite some brainstorming on your part before you start to make your video.

What you need to make a successful YouTube video

In terms of technical equipment when you make a YouTube (or a web video) you need a laptop or PC and a good quality webcam. Webcams, these days, are good enough to make the success of your video hinge on the content, rather than the quality of the video itself.

If you want to go up one, do some research and pick up one of the latest breed of cameras which can shoot video which can be downloaded straight to your hard drive (or use PlayStation 3 the web cam of which allows you to upload straight to YouTube).

If you are looking for tips which can make your web video production slicker (in order to infuse an entertainment factor in them) the website videomaker (http://www.videomaker.com/youtube/) contains some great tips and hints which can help you turn out some pretty professional video. Do bear in mind that honesty and directness however still sell and this is proven in the same website where they use a relatively low-key video to show some pretty slick effects (just a guy talking to a camera): http://www.videomaker.com/video/watch/tips-and-tricks/494/gun-muzzle-flashes-andblast-sounds/

Bear in mind that the simplicity of direct delivery works well even in super slick video productions as our next example illustrates.

How Old Spice revitalized a tired brand with a web viral campaign

Unless you were born before the 60s chances are that Old Spice is the aftershave your dad or granddad used and which, to a male child's mind then, stood for a sign of growing up and being able to use yourself.

This is how old and troubled the brand was. It had a product which had not changed almost since Noah stepped out of the Ark and a target population which perceived it as tired and old-worldly.

Then, in 2010 the company launched a series of thirty second ads which on YouTube they went viral. The very first one currently has over 27 million views and can be seen here: http://www.youtube.com/watch?v=owGykVbfgUE

The direct talking to the camera, the entertainment factor of the video which makes it fun to watch and, fortuitously, the noise which the ads created after they first appeared (a bet was made during a live show whether they used CGI or it was all done in one scene – a video which itself produced over 1.5 million additional views: http://www.youtube.com/watch?v=VDk9jjdiXJQ), as they were shared on Facebook and passed along through Twitter, gave the company the idea to make impromptu videos which addressed individual Twitter users in a one-to-one video.

The results? According to online video metrics specialist, Visual Measures, the campaign rapidly became "one of the fastest growing online video campaigns of all time." The results of the campaign were impressive, with 183 videos made in total, 11 million views, and over 22,000 comments in three days.

By the time they had finished they had made over 200 videos talking, individually to celebrities like Hollywood actress Alyssa Milano (http://www.youtube.com/watch?v=s5KIYhXa_8E&feature=player_embedded) or web personalities like Kevin Rose (founder of Digg.com) who upon Twitting that he was not feeling well received the following personalized message on YouTube: http://www.youtube.com/watch?v=So5yDtITswY.

The message then prompted Kevin Rose to Twit to his over 1 million followers: *HOLY SH*T, best get* *well video EVER from the old spice man!*: http://bit.ly/dpSeOs

The link appeared on the social news sharing website www.digg.com where it received enough votes to make it to the site's first page which itself brought hundreds of thousands of visitors to the Old Spice website.

Old Spice however expanded the campaign to include ordinary Twitter users. The real aim of the campaign was to overhaul the brand and bring a tired, 'old' brand into a hip-hop modern internet age. Subsequently figures also showed that Old Spice sales doubled following the Twitter video campaign.

Reading this I know that you are thinking, OK, good for them but how can I achieve the same effect when I am not a Corporation? Well, the principle which helped Old Spice achieve their goals is the same. In order to succeed in the real-time web and produce lasting impact in terms of marketing, branding and sales, with the greatest potential to go viral you really need to have:

1. A good mix of real-time and traditional internet tools (Old Spice used Twitter to drive traffic to their YouTube videos which then led people to their website).
2. A campaign which is entertaining and can become personalized (like the Old Spice videos showed).
3. A product or a service which is great in quality.
4. An understanding of how to throw it all together in the mix.

In the 21st century the real-time web is in a constant state of flux with audiences flowing along trends and always looking for the next best thing which will excite them. Most corporations (Old Spice who were desperate, excluded) display the same kind of inability to move fast as shown by United Airlines when Dave Carroll first made his (they did nothing) or, even more recently BP's inability to respond to Twitter attacks on the oil spill disaster in the Gulf of Mexico (it was weeks before they even began to get a Twitter campaign of communication in place and even then it was woefully inadequate and the damage had been done).

This makes you, the individual who 'gets it' suddenly powerful. Create a video which has all the right ingredients, publicize it on Facebook and Twitter, stay on top of it in terms of responses and you can suddenly find yourself reaping the rewards of the next viral campaign.

I end this chapter with one addition. If you want to track the success of your video marketing across the web you may want to start using video analytics (either the free or paid-for formats) provided by TubeMogul http://www.tubemogul.com. It will give you the same analysis ability you enjoy on your website with Google Analytics so that you can more closely track the effectiveness of your online video campaigns. If you only upload video to YouTube the free Google video Analytics service Insight (http://www.youtube.com/t/advertising_insight) will do much the same thing.

Finally, if you are using video (and you should) you need to know how to successfully optimize it for search engines. Appendix 4, at the back of this book, gives you all the practical steps you need to take into account there.

Chapter #8
Niche not mass

The biggest thing in niche marketing is not just getting the one guy who appeals to one particular group. But getting the guy that resonates deeply with the general market. That way you get a double hit because everybody in the general market appreciates him. **Nathaniel Mason**

The very premise of the internet is not that it globalized markets. This is a perception that's a natural by-product of its reach. What it did from the very beginning and what it continues to do and what the real-time web is a natural focus of is the fact that it took personalized marketing and made it global. This is a fine distinction. Those who do not really understand the web tend to think that because the web gives you access to a global population of hundreds of millions that's also the potential size of your target group. That's wrong. The web made it possible to increase the niche market by allowing us to market to enough individuals, either locally or globally to make almost any niche market suddenly viable.

That is the single largest paradigm shift in online marketing.

It is also what will guide, in nine out of ten cases, the success of your real-time web efforts. If you are not targeting a specific group of people with a very specific product you are diffusing your marketing efforts to the point that they will really have very little real impact on your target market and will simply become additional background noise on the web.

Making sure you have a niche

Interestingly enough one of the commonest subjects I receive emails about is just how to find your niche. This comes from people who feel they have skills, knowledge and professional experience to contribute but are unsure in what direction to channel it all into.

Finding your niche deserves, most probably, a book all on its own. If you look online for help in finding a niche you will find countless of websites which tell you to do some keyword research in order to determine what is popular with online searchers in particular fields and start to narrow down and focus on them.

This is not just a little wrong. It is, quite literally, putting the horse before the cart and hoping it can pull it. Keyword research is an SEO tool (like the ones I listed in my best-selling book: *SEO Help: 20 steps to get your website to the #1 page of Google*) and little different in terms of practical bias than any of the real-time web tools we have listed in this book. Using it to find your market niche is a little like using the telescope, looking at the stars and thinking they are planets. Without anything to hang the knowledge you uncover on you are only more likely to make serious mistakes in how you interpret it and use it.

If you really want to find your niche your best friend is a plain piece of paper and a pen. Divide it into two and on one half write down all the things you are really good at and on the second put down all the things you wish you could do as a business in which you are the boss.

Be exhaustive and detailed and see what clicks. Do not expect miracles. This is a process of elimination and what comes out first is the garbage, which is good. If nothing comes of the first piece of paper start another. Again go through the process until you have run out of skills and things you want to do. Keep both pieces of paper.

Now take a third.

Put in it, in a single column all the things you wish existed in the world. This is free-floating thinking at its best. It produced internet business success stories such as the Lucky Break Wishbone Company (http://www.luckybreakwishbone.com/) and Alex Tew's Million Dollar Homepage (http://milliondollarhomepage.com/) which netted him close to a million dollars.

It is only after you have found a niche into which you can channel your passion that you will then be able to successfully use all the tools we have been looking ta here, to help market it.

On the web passion is what drives success and not the other way around and those who have, for one reason or another, managed to be successful by accident without really having a true passion for what they do, fade without making much of a mark, their concentration and energies absorbed by things other than their business.

Chapter #9

The year of SEO

Every webmaster and every website owner wants the same thing: to see their website on Google's first page and to keep it there. **David Amerland**

The web marks its development through one thing and one thing only: data. Data is incontrovertible in terms of the evidence it provides and it tends to form its own mileposts.

2010 was the year Facebook served more data than Google and overtook Google in terms of the length of time people spend there. It was the year Google became the leading search engine on the web by stint that now, in practice, we could see that the amalgamation of Yahoo! and BING produced a hybrid which was actually weaker than each of those search engines had been on their own. It was the year when the real-time web really took off and SEO, social marketing, branding and online marketing finally converged like separate strands being twisted into a single length of rope.

While I have used the term real-time web throughout this book to signify the development the web is undergoing towards immediacy and real-time responses, each of the trends and tools we have covered here are really intended to help you do one thing: to successfully market your online business.

In this regard, they differ little from SEO and indeed, in my book on the subject: *SEO Help: 20 steps to get your website to Google's #1 page*, I detail many practical techniques which utilize social media and real-time web services to help increase a website's visibility, to the same end.

2011 can be rightly called the 'Year of SEO' because many of the activities which require next to no programming skills and which are routinely performed as part of a website's online marketing are now, also, part of its SEO activities, which help the same website to rank high on the organic search engine results pages (SERPs).

Success in online visibility is now slowly moving away from the hands of 'specialists' who rightly should only be brought in if there is no time to perform specific tasks, to the hands of website owners. This means that it is now imperative to conceptually take this into account so when you plan your website's activities and its content you also think along the needs of SEO and optimization in the full meaning of the word.

The web has always been, to me, the great equalizer. The means through which the individual can leverage the same kind of exposure and success as a giant corporation in order to achieve his dreams. The time for this right now. The tools we need to make it happen are all present and all it requires is that we understand each and how to use it.

Other real-time web tools at your disposal

Just because we focused on Twitter, Facebook and MySpace as prime examples of real-time web strategies does not mean that that's all there is.

The popularity of these services means that they are, in the list of priorities of real-time web tools to use, in the top slots. Their existence and popularity, however, are the direct results of a trend which has been present since the web first became what it is, back in 1995, and we simply did not have the technology to achieve it.

This means that there are other, slightly older, tools you should be using which are also a vital aspect of any online promotional strategy and which can, in their own way, also help broaden the reach of your online business. While each of the ones we will look at now are relatively old in terms of existence it is only the latest advances in web programming which have allowed their integration in the real-time web and the immediate access it provides to goods and services.

The first of these is chat and its integration in websites (as well as its presence on Facebook) as a means of reaching the site owner and getting information about a point of interest on the website, fast. Chat has been around for some time now and developed naturally from the very early days of the web and its chatrooms. Today's chat programs allow a fairly seamless integration in a website with the intent to allow those who come to it to quickly ask any questions they may have and reach an actionable decision much faster.

When handled properly chat on a website gives you the opportunity to directly interact with a potential customer and help overcome any residual barriers there may be to a purchasing decision.

Chat software available to you

The list which follows is by no means exhaustive of the subject and a Google search will provide many more solutions. It is a good start however which will save you a lot of time and money and it is more than possible that the solution you are looking for is already included in the list.

1. Crafty Syntax (http://www.craftysyntax.com**) -** The Crafty Syntax powered chat is a PHP programmed service that at no cost can be installed in an external website. The software offers a good customization level that lets you adjust many aspects of it, you can also monitor the visitors and chat sessions while chatting with more than one person, which can be done in a single tab. In addition you can execute a complete traffic analysis to determine the exact origin of your site's traffic, another advantage of the service is the fact that you can see what the visitors are typing as they're typing their message to you so you can prepare in advance with your replies.

2. Zopim (http://www.zopim.com) - This site provides a top quality chat service that goes from a lite version at no cost to a business subscription with all the features included. Among the benefits of using Zopim is the end of pop-up windows, create automated messages, get complete traffic analysis of your live visitors, rank your costumers so you can always assist the most important clients and finally, trigger-based chats. The lite version is free and can be upgraded to different versions [solo (9 USD/month), solo plus (15 USD/month), team (39 USD/month) and business (99 USD/month)].

3. Comm100 (http://www.comm100.com/livechat) -

This is probably one of the best chat services available, mostly because it covers almost all the functions of paid services at no cost. You can insert a live chat application inside your website to start getting in touch with your visitors. It also has a fully customizable capacity so you can edit things such as the chat button, chat window, pre-chat and offline message. This service is multi-lingual and currently offers English, Spanish, German and Japanese support. Also you can customize your different chat styles from one site to another. It's important to mention that this is a hosted and open-source service.

4. BoldChat (http://www.boldchat.com/) - BoldChat is software technology made specifically for increasing website sales and improving customer service. It's not free and its price range goes from 29 to 199 USD per month. This is a fully integrated customer relationship management (CRM) service with features which include proactive chat invitations, full customization, visitors monitoring, email management and much more. The cost may be prohibitive and, like everything else you implement online, you will need to balance it against the value each purchase brings in, in order to decide.

5. Olark (http://www.olark.com/portal/tour) - Founded by a group of people from Palo Alto, CA. Olark is a paid live chat service whose prices range from 15 to 149 USD per month. Among the services that they provide is the capacity to use multiple operators and compatibility with digital devices such as laptops, iPhone and Blackberry. Other services include sending offline messages and complete visual customization, easy integration with your website, international support and the ability to analyze your visitors' statistics in real time.

6.   Chatterous   (http://www.chatterous.com)   – Chatterous, as the name suggests, is live chat software that can be used from the web, IM, email or even the phone. Some of the features provided by this service are easy integration with popular communications tools and no registration required. In general terms this is a useful tool which allows you to offer chat implementation on your website.

7. Live Chat Now (http://www.livechatnow.com) - This is a paid for service, which at 19.50 USD per month includes an extended list of services, such as group conversations, a preset library, auto answer, chat history, visitor's transferring, live spelling/auto correction, auto invitations customized buttons and more.

8.   Volusion   (http://www.volusion.com/live-chat/software.asp) - Volusion is a web company that offers a lot of services which include live chat, which comes in two different presentations, the Basic Live Chat (free) and the Premium Live Chat (29.95 USD / operator). Some of the features of the Volusion chat include incoming alerts of new chat requests, "other person is typing" indicator, tabbed windows for multiple   chats,   online/offline   status   message,

Page107

customers can email when you're offline, customizable chat icons and Volusion branding below the Click-To-Chat Icon.

9. CustomerReach
(http://www.customerreach.com/default.aspx) - With CustomerReach, you can choose the live chat service or run your own live chat server. You can start with a free account and upgrade up to a one time license fee starting at $399.00 USD. This live chat software gives users the opportunity to chat with their customers while they're visiting the website in order to provide help and support; it also allows companies to track, monitor and communicate with their website visitors in real-time, another service is that it comes with on-board analytics which allow you to check the origin of the visitor and the keywords they had used to arrive to your website.

10. PHPOpenChat (http://www.phpopenchat.org) - PHPOpenChat is a high performance PHP-based free chat server software for a live chat-room or -module which can be integrated on every PHP-based site. At this time you can integrate this chat software into postnuke, phpbb, yabbse, as a module. Like most open source products its development schedule is a little unpredictable. Once in a while the developers of this chat provider release new bug fixes and updates that are designed to improve the capacity of the implementation.

11. OCC (http://www.onlinechatcenters.com) – This is a powerful chat tool The OCC chat provider offers a free version of its chat that perfectly covers most companies' needs, making it a top choice to support your business, although you can upgrade to the premium version paying the amount of 29.95 USD per year. In the free account are included multiple operators, the ability to handle multiple websites, chat invitations, web and desktop apps, stored messages, customizable chat request form, email signature, operator rating system, real-time mouse tracking for co-browsing the Premium version is even more powerful.

12. Website Alive (http://www.websitealive.com) - One of the most famous chat services on the internet, WebsiteAlive is a powerful tool that you can try by registering to the 10 days free-trial, after that the subscription prices oscillate from 29.95 USD to 97.95 USD per month. Some of the best features of this live chat are a list of dynamic buttons, which, depending on the online status of your Operators, your "Live Chat Support Button" will change and your visitors will know immediately if you're available for chatting. You can also send a chat transcript to any email address, capture leads when you're offline, search and filter previous chat.

13. Ogg Chat (http://oggchat.com) - Ogg Chat is paid-for, live chat software that integrates with Gmail and Gtalk. You can have a 14 day free-trial after which, if you like what you have seen, you can go

ahead and register for one of their plans. Prices go from 9.95 USD to more than 39.95 USD per month.
The chat software incorporates features such as live visitor monitoring, live chat history, IP tracking, and customizable chat windows, but routes all chats directly to each operator's Google Talk account. This means operators don't need special software or training, they just have to access their Gmail account or their IM client of choice and start accepting and answering customer chat requests.

14. HelpCenter (http://www.helpcenterlive.com) - Help Center Live is an open-source live chat system. Because of its open-source nature, this chat service provider is being constantly updated and bugs are fixed as they are reported. It is powerful but needs trialing before you can decide if it's right for you.

15. LiveZilla (http://livehelp.livezilla.net/home/en) - LiveZilla is a free chat service featuring many useful features which include an integrated real-time visitor monitoring feature that allows you to see instantly who is on your site and fully customizable chat elements. LiveZilla also runs on your own web server, with no subsequent payments and 100% control over your data; the software is able to resolve Geo Location (based on IP-to-location) for the visitors on your website, further personalizing their experience. Another potentially useful consideration is that it comes with webcam support for more personalized chats.

16. LiveChat Volusion for Joomla (http://extensions.joomla.org/extensions/communication/live-support-hosted/7755) – This is a non-commercial extension for the award-winning Open Source CMS, Joomla. It will set up a chat inside your website so you can start chatting with your visitors.

The free extension is for s ingle operator but you can have multiple operators if you buy their Premium Edition.

17. OneClickChat (http://www.oneclickchat.com) - OneClickChat offers a timely and cost-effective solution to the issue of communicating live with your website visitors. You can choose either the Personal Edition which has zero cost or the Professional that costs 9.99 USD per month. Some of the features that this service offers are: Live interaction with your site visitors using a powerful rich-text chat application, transfer calls from one operator to another to improve your customer service, the ability to customize and use multiple configurations and languages for the button images and chat window, being able to determine and use your own canned answers to save time when chatting with the visitors, being able to see in real-time comprehensive information about your web site visitors, like where they are on the current web page and the time spent on each page and so on.

18. Plupper (http://plupper.com/index.xhtml) - Plupper is an integrated single point of contact software which makes communication with customers or web page visitors simple. It is a paid-for service with a cost of up to 2,999 USD for the dedicated service though there is also a free subscription with more limited functionality you can try out. The Plupper Widget is currently available in more than 10 different languages, including English, Spanish and French. Plupper integrates smoothly with GTalk, you only need to set your Google account name in the operator settings page, all chats with operators are saved and stored so you can search and browse your chat history whenever you like. With the Geo-location service you can locate any website visitor on the map with impressive accuracy.

19.   Shine   Live   Help (http://shinelivehelp.sourceforge.net) - This is an improved version of Crafty Syntax. Shine Live Help is an open source chat software for website sales and support. It works as a standalone chat and integrates with Sugar Open Source CRM. Source code for this project may be available as downloads or through one of the SCM repositories used by the project, as well as being accessible from the project developer's page.

20. UZoom (http://www.uzoom.com) - Live Chat software by UZoom focuses on combining cutting edge technology and powerful customer service to provide the best possible professional live chat services. You can find a useful data field on the site where some of the most relevant live chat providers are analyzed and it will help you to execute a thoughtful analysis. Their live chat service can be downloaded by simply copying and pasting a few lines of HTML code into your website.

More real-time services

The trend towards real-time on the web means that there are two underlying tendencies being experienced by website visitors and programmers alike. The former feel the need for as many means to contact a website operator easily and quickly and the latter look for ways to seamlessly integrate applications so that they are not entirely standalone any more.

What this means in practical terms is that when you do have a website and when you do create Facebook Pages you need to provide as many different ways for visitors to reach you as you can. This includes phone numbers, email, live chat and Skype.

In terms of integration services such as Skype now allow you to import your Facebook friends and use Skype to connect with them and Skype itself has a news stream and a status which mirrors in functionality Facebook's Wall.

Provided you are aware of the tendency for multiple ways to be reached and the overall integration which is allowing different web applications to 'talk' to each other, and take advantage of the trend to benefit your business it is unlikely that potential customers will find it difficult to do business with you.

David Amerland

01010100011000010110101101100101001000000011
11001011011110111010101110010001000000011011
11011011100110110001101001011011100110010100010
010000001101101011000010111001001101011001101010110
01010111010001101001011011100110011100100000
00111010001101111001000000110001001000000001
10110001100101011101100110010101101100001000
00001110111011010000110010101110010011001010
00100000001111001011011110111010100100000011
00011011000010110111000100000001110100011011
1101110100011000010110110001101100011110010
010000001100011011011110110111001110100000111
001001101111011011000010000000110100101110100
000101110

Chapter #10

The Last Word

The illiterate of the 21st century will not be those who cannot read and write, but those who cannot learn, unlearn, and relearn. **Alvin Toffler**

Final chapters are funny things. They tend to either recap what's been said before in a book or tell you about something which is almost-so, simply because now is the time to know about it.

Here, I will do neither.

The chapters which have preceded this are packed with the tools you need to make your online business successful and to make your online presence visible, active, and fully integrated in the web of today.

The thing to remember about working online is that the medium is in a constant state of flux. Take the tools and use them but do not be wedded to them. There will be more tools which will come along tomorrow and it is always best to be able to make the choices which serve you best.

In all the years I have been online I have never lost a sense of excitement at the potential thrown up by the web. I became involved in eBook publishing at the turn of last century, when it was way too premature to do so, because I was excited by the potential. I have remained active at the forefront of the web because I simply love what it can do and love what it stands for.

Whatever you do online, however you do it, it should light you up. If you do not feel the passion of what you do fire you up in the morning as you get out of bed, chances are that your online venture will fail. While it is true that the online world is full of opportunity and possibilities, it is also true that it is full of competition. Whatever idea you may have, someone else is also having (or worse, having a better one than you).

In order to get ahead in this game you need to feel the overriding passion which allows you to go the extra mile, stay up the extra hour, and work at your marketing that little bit extra.

I have been advising business and individuals long enough to know that passion is the missing ingredient to success. When that is not there the excuses which crop up on why things did not happen and why plans did not work would fill tomes.

There are many times when I have stayed up late at night, fuelled by strong coffee, eyes smarting from too many hours looking at a screen, carrying out a bit more research, working on yet a little more analysis, testing one more hypothesis on how interaction between applications affects a website's marketing, when I should be sleeping or being out with friends.

Lack of sleep and sacrifice on personal time is the price we pay for the knowledge we need and success we chase.

Should you ever find yourself in that position, should you be at your computer, fighting back fatigue and forcing yourself to keep on working, think that you are in good company. There are countless of us out there, working individually, creating the web we want to be part of.

To you, and all others, I raise a proverbial mug of coffee. The future of marketing on the web belongs to you all.

Finally, on a few pages of the book I have left, for the adventurous, a binary, fun marketing message. If you have some time and do not mind typing a bunch of '1s' and '0s' head over to http://www.roubaixinteractive.com/PlayGround/Binary_Conversion/Binary_To_Text.asp and decode the numbers into text.

Best of success in your endeavors!

Appendix 1
How to ask effective questions on Twitter

Twitter is a great place for conversation, fact-finding and the testing of ideas, provided, of course, you can phrase everything in terms which will get your audience fired up and be willing to participate. This is what this guide is all about:

Keep questions on topic
The types of questions you should ask on Twitter will depend upon the way you normally use the microblogging website. If you use it in a personal way then, almost any question will work but if your use of Twitter is more focused upon exploring a topic or niche related to your business then – you'll want to keep your questions focused within your topic because those who follow you will expect just that.

Acknowledge answers

Simply asking questions and ignoring the answers sends the message that you simply do not care what anybody thinks and you cannot even be bothered to reply. If you are really successful with your question the chances are you will get quite a few replies which make it difficult to then respond personally to them.

In that case some of the following tips will help:

- Post a general 'thanks for your answers' type tweet.
- Pick a few good responses to retweet and highlight as key answers.
- Use answers publicly – for example you could pull the answers together and use them (or at least some of them) in a blog post which then gives value to the effort of all those who replied to your question.

Be willing to answer your own questions

When it comes to questions you should always be prepared to put your money where your mouth is by joining the conversation yourself. Not only does this guarantee that your followers feel they can get hold of you but they also get to know more about your ideas and approach to the issues you post about.

Monitor what you put online

Make sure that you monitor your questions (which means that when you do post them you should be ready to reply to anything which is said as a response. This allows you not just to show that you are engaged

Page 119

and able to respond in real-time (which is why the real-time web is so addictive in the first instance) but also that you truly care about the responses you get and the opinion of those who respond.

Leave Space for Answers and Conversation
In Twitter you only have 140 characters so space is not just an issue you need to deal with, it has to also be part of your online strategy which means that you must leave space for retweets so that those who retweet your Tweets can also add comments. You should also leave space between Tweets. Sending out 15 Tweets an hour barely gives your followers time to think, reply and post, all of which create the engagement you seek. So make sure you keep your Tweets short and your posts at no more than one an hour.

Appendix 2

How to create a Facebook profile page you can use to market your business

Step 1. Register your account. Go to Facebook (www.facebook.com) . In the top right of the screen on the blue task bar, click on 'Register'. You'll be taken to a registration screen. Put in your name, select what it is you do - i.e. are you a businessman? Next enter a valid email address. This is so that Facebook can contact you for confirmation of your registration and in future send you updates from your profile. Next enter a password of your choice and your birthday (notice that you do not have to fill this in). Then enter the weird text you see in the security check into the text box beneath it. Agree to the terms and conditions, and click 'Register now'.

Step 2. Confirm your email. Facebook will now tell you it has sent a confirmation email to your email account. You must now login to your email. Open the confirmation email from Facebook, click on the link it provides and it will take you to you new Facebook profile.

Step 3. Find friends and contacts. You'll now have to go through a series of steps to personalize your profile. First, Facebook will offer to scour your email address book for people who are on Facebook who you can invite to be your friends. Simply enter your email address and password, and Facebook will find your friends. Remember that this is all done for business so select the ones you want to add by ticking the boxes to the left of their pictures, and then click 'add to friends' at the bottom. Then you'll be able to choose friends from your email address book who aren't on Facebook and send an email to them inviting them to join up and be your friend. If you have business contacts or acquaintances you have not updated on your activities for some time and you have not been quite sure how to start, this is a golden opportunity. One of the benefits of marketing through Facebook is that when it is done right it feels more like games and socializing and less like marketing, which makes it easier to break down barriers and reach those you want to reach.

Step 4. Find contacts. Classmates might be an easy one to start with, remember though this is a business account so again be careful who you end up adding to it. A guy from school who used to harass you, for instance, may not be the best choice no matter how nostalgic or curious you are. Click on 'Find my classmates'. First select the country, city, and the name of your school, and the class year. If you are searching for a specific person, type in their name. Click 'Search for classmates'. Now select anyone you recognize or want to add as a friend and click 'Add to friends'. Sometimes when you add a friend, you'll have to write the text from the security box into the text box to confirm. You can also search by your college or university by putting in the name of the college, the year, and a classmate name if you like.

Step 5. Find workmates. Click on 'Search for your co-workers'. Write the name of the company you are looking for and the name of the employee if necessary. The click 'Search for co-workers' to see who Facebook can find (also try this if you are trying to connect with people who work with companies you want to start business with).

Step 6. Join a regional network. You cannot view other people's profiles if you are not friends with each other, unless you are both in the same regional network. Joining a regional network means it's easier to track down friends and it becomes easier to start forming a social network you can leverage to help your business. On your Facebook setup homepage, there is the option to enter a city or town. Put in your home city and click 'Join'.

Step 7. Edit your profile. Next click on 'My profile'. You'll see that there all the sections are empty.

Basic - Click 'Edit' and you will be able to enter personal details about yourself. To begin with enter your basic details. Select your sex, whether you are interested in men or women, your relationship status, and what you are on Facebook for. You can state 'Friendship', 'Dating', 'A relationship', or, in our case 'Networking'. Next select your birthday, hometown, state (if you live in one) and describe your religious views – remember that when it comes to religious and political views they may be business deal-breakers, so make sure you keep this neutral, uncritical and non-facetious . Once you have filled in all the fields you are comfortable filling in, click 'save changes'. Don't forget, you can always go back and edit your details whenever you want.

Contact - Next click on 'Contact' in the tabs bar. Here you can add a screen name that people will see when they view your profile. If you like, you can enter your phone number. Remember, Facebook is public, so think before you enter certain personal information but do enter information which makes it easy for them to contact your business if they are interested.
Remember that only those who become added to your friends will be able to view it though. You can also enter your address and city of residence. If you live in the states, you can stick in your state. Also put in your website (this one is a must). Then click 'Save changes'.

Personal - Next click on 'Personal' in the tabs bar. Here you can enter Activities, Interests, Favorite music, Favorite TV shows, Favorite music, Favorite books, Favorite quotes, and fill out an 'About me' section. Most people enter stuff as a list - but bear in mind, the longer it is, the less likely people are to read it. So if you do want to make your Facebook profile reflect your personality and your business, and you want people to read it, then keep it short and interesting and relevant. Click 'Save changes' when you are done

Education - If click on the 'Education' tab - you can enter your school or college and the year you graduated. This will help other people from your school find you. This is useful if you think your erstwhile classmates might be looking for you in terms of work or services and, it never hurts to leverage past connections for business.

Work - Next click on the 'work' tab and, if you like, enter information about where you work, a description of your job, and the length of time you have worked there. Remember, you don't have to fill out every field. But if you do enter your place of work, it will be easier for people to find you if they search for your workplace.

Picture - Then click on the 'Picture' tab. Here you can upload a picture from your hard drive that other people will be able to see as your profile picture. Click 'Browse', find a picture on your hard drive, tick the box to certify that you own the rights to the image, then click 'Upload picture'. Remember again that this is a business account. Try to make the picture interesting because being eye-catching will lead to more clicks on your profile but do not make it silly, light-hearted or anything which might work against you in terms of business.

That's it. You're done! You have a Facebook profile page which can now be used to launch your Facebook business presence.

Appendix 3
How to create a customized Facebook Fan Page

These are often used to promote deals, call attention to new products, or simply welcome visitors with an attractive branded splash page. Anyone with a Fan Page can create one, but it takes a little effort. Here's how.

1. Add the Static FBML App

The tabs at the top of your Facebook Fan Page are applications (apps for short). Some, like your wall and photos are built into Facebook. Others are essentially plug-ins where fans can view external content which you may have posted on rich media sites such as YouTube (videos), Flickr (photos) and so on.

The application you need for your custom page is called "Static FBML," if you need to find it on Facebook it is located here: http://www.facebook.com/apps/application.php?id=4 949752878 You need to be logged into Facebook go to it and then choose to add it to your Page (a pop-up dialogue box will allow you to choose where you want to add it to). The application is essentially a blank canvas where you can add whatever content you want, including custom graphics and links via standard HTML.

2. Set Up Your Tab

Once you've added the Static FBML app, click "Edit Page" below your Fan Page's profile image. This will bring up all your settings and apps. Look for the FBML app and click the "Application Settings" link.

The application can function in two ways: As a set of boxes, or as one dedicated profile tab. If you're building a splash page, you'll probably want to use it as a tab, so go ahead and make sure that the "Box" setting is removed, and the "Tab" setting is added. You can always experiment with boxes later if you find them more useful.

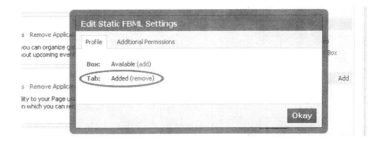

3. Add Your Content

Once you're in tab mode, go back to your settings and click the "Edit" link under the Static FBML app. This opens a standard text field where you can add your content.

"Box Title" will be the default name of your tab, so you'll want to change it to something appropriate, like "This Week's Deal," "Special Offers," or simply "Welcome," with an explanation of what the Page actually does. It really depends on how you plan to use your Page.

The main text field is where your content goes, and you can add standard HTML to the page as you would any website, including images, text, links, and other formatting. No need for HTML, BODY, or HEAD tags.

Note that your images must be hosted elsewhere (on your company's website, for example) and only referenced in your HTML code.

4. Make It the Default Landing Page

If you want this new tab to be the "face" of your business Fan Page, head back over to your page settings and edit your "Wall Settings." There is an option for "Default Landing Tab for Everyone Else." From that menu, select your new tab.

From now on, it will be the first thing visitors see when they arrive.

5. Engage Further With FBML

FBML stands for Facebook Markup Language, and it is the code used in Facebook applications to reference items on the social network, like user profiles, groups, feeds, and other data. If you're really looking to integrate your landing page and get interactive with visitors, it might be worthwhile to learn the basics of this language. If time is of an issue (when is it not ever?) you may want to consider buying a ready-made FBML template and customizing it to suit your needs.

A quick Google search will give you many of the websites which now sell ready-made Facebook FBML templates. Costs range from as little as $15 to a couple of hundred, depending on your requirements, uniqueness, level of customization required and so on.

Appendix 4
How to optimise video to rank high on search engines

The steps below give you everything you need in order to make sure that your videos are easy to find through search engines.

1. Optimize Everything: When it comes to optimizing your video, you want to pay special attention to your Title, Description, Tags, and Captions/Annotations. The more keyword-rich and engaging you can make them, the better.

2. Test your Thumbnails: Once you upload your video, YouTube will allow you to pick from three video stills to use as that video's thumbnail image. You may want to test what works best for you. Does a human face get more clicks than a slate of text? Does a smiling woman get more clicks than an image of your CEO (probably)? These are things you'll want to experiment with to make sure picking the thumbnail that will lead to the most conversions.

3. Add Transcripts: A transcript file must be saved as a plain text file without any special characters like smartquotes or emdashes.
Here's what a transcript might look like:

>> FISHER: All right. So, let's begin. This session is: Going Social

with the YouTube APIs. I am Jeff Fisher,

and this is Johann Hartmann, we're presenting today.

[pause]

YouTube uses experimental speech recognition technology to provide automatic timing for your English transcript. Automatic timing creates a caption file that you can download. Short videos with good sound quality and clear spoken English synchronize best.

Here are some other things you can do to help get the best automatic timing results for your transcripts:

Identify long pauses (3 seconds or longer) or music in the transcript with a double line break.

Use double line breaks anytime you want to force a caption break.

Here are some common captioning practice that help readability:

Descriptions inside square brackets like [music] or [laughter] can help people with hearing disabilities to understand what is happening in your video.

You can also add tags like >> at the beginning of a new line to identify speakers or change of speaker. YouTube allows you to upload the transcript file you have created and saved in a notepad .txt file format to the video through the 'Add Caption or Transcript' option. The advantage of any transcript is that in a long video it allows the entire content to suddenly become capable of being indexed by search engines.

4. End with a call to action: Make sure your video closes with some type of call to action. If someone sat there and watched your entire two minute video should be able to do something by the end of it. Include a call to action that encourages them to continue their interaction with your brand and gets them to DO something, whether it's to visit your site, check out a blog post or even to share the video with their friends. If you're not including a call to action at the end of your video, you're missing out on a great marketing opportunity.

5. Make an offer: Want to increase views and comments on your video? Offer an incentive for customers to do so. Maybe there's a free discount

Page 133

code in the video or something that will give them special access to your brand. Include an offer to incentivize the video.

6. Make it easy to share: Encourage people to share your video by including calls to action for them to do so, uploading it on Facebook and, of course, tweeting it! The new version of Twitter is designed to put media right in the forefront of the service. That means prime real estate for your video content.

7. Experiment with different platforms: While it's the biggest, YouTube isn't the only video game in town. Try uploading your video content to sites like Vimeo, Viddler, Blip.tv, iTunes and others to increase your audience and monopolize more room on the search engines results page. When you upload your content to both YouTube and another platform, you can make them both rank for keyword-searches. Don't have time to upload the same video to multiple sites? TubeMogul (www.tubemogul.com) will do it for you at no cost.

8. Alter the content for each platform: Or, instead of uploading the same content to different platforms, tailor the content to the different audiences to increase conversion rates. This may not always be possible but it certainly should be part of your thinking and planning process for the creation of video content.

9. Put videos on high-conversion pages: Help increase sales by using online video on conversion pages. This is a technique which more and more websites successfully use, including the use of video right on the Homepage and on those pages which attract the most traffic.

10. Create playlists: If you've ever gotten stuck in an endless loop on YouTube watching one funny video after another, you know that video is addictive. Luckily, it's also addictive for your customers. Help feed their addiction by creating playlists for them to watch and subscribe to. By going to your My Videos page and linking your videos, you help your customers kill their entire day watching content about your brand.

Social Media Marketing: 101 Terms you need to know

A

Application Programing Interface (API) - An API is a documented interface that allows one software application to to interact with another application. An example of this is the Twitter API.

Avatar - An Avatar is an image or username that represents a person online within forums and social networks.

B

BackType (www.backtype.com) - BackType is a social media analytics company that helps companies measure their social engagement. Previously the service started as a blog comment search engine.

Bit.ly (www.bit.ly) - Bit.ly is a free URL shortening service that provides statistics for the links users share online. Bit.ly is popularly used to condense long URLs to make them easier to share on social networks such as Twitter.

Blip.TV (www.blip.tv) - Blip.TV is an online video sharing site that provides a free and paid platform for anyone who hosts an online video show.

Blog - Blog is a word that was created from two words: "web log". Blogs are usually maintained by an individual with regular entries of commentary, descriptions of events, or other material such as graphics or video. Entries are commonly displayed in reverse-chronological order. "Blog" can also be used as a verb, meaning *to maintain or add content to a blog*.

Blogger (www.blogger.com) - Blogger is a free blogging platform owned by Google that allows individuals and companies to host and publish a blog typically on a subdomain. Example: yourblogname.blogspot.com

Blog Talk Radio (www.blogtalkradio.com) - Blog Talk Radio is a free web application that allows users to host live online radio shows.

BoardReader (www.boardreader.com)   -
BoardReader is a free search engine that allows users to search for keywords only in posts and titles of online forums, a popular forum of social networking.

Boxee (www.boxee.tv) - Boxee is a social video application that allows users to watch online videos on their TVs and computers. Users can share and watch videos from a variety of online videos sources for free.

C

Chat- Chat can refer to any kind of communication over the Internet, but traditionally refers to one-to-one communication through a text-based chat application commonly referred to as instant messaging applications.

Collecta (www.collecta.com) - Collecta is a real-time search engine that includes results from from blogs, microblogs, news feeds and photo sharing services as they are published.

Collective Intelligence - Collective Intelligence is a shared or group intelligence that emerges from the collaboration and competition of many individuals and appears in consensus decision-making in social networks.

Comment - A comment is a response that is often provided as an answer of reaction to a blog post or message on a social network. Comments are a primary form of two-way communication on the social web.

Compete (www.compete.com) - Compete is a web-based application that offers users and businesses web analytics and enables people to compare and contrast the statistics for different websites over time.

Craigslist (www.craigslist.org) - Craigslist is a popular online commerce site in which users sell a variety of goods and services to other users. The service has been credited for causing the reduction of classified advertising in newspapers across the United States.

Creative Commons (www.creativecommons.org) - Creative Commons is a nonprofit corporation dedicated to making it easier for people to share and build upon the work of others, consistent with the rules of copyright. It provides free licenses and other legal tools to mark creative work with the freedom the creator wants it to carry, so others can share, remix, use commercially, or any combination thereof.

D

Delicious (www.delicious.com) - Delicious is a free online bookmarking service that lets users save website addresses publicly and privately online so that they can be accessed from any device connected to the Internet and shared with friends.

Digg (www.digg.com) - Digg is a social news website that allows members to submit and vote for articles. Articles with the most votes appear on the homepage of the site and subsequently are seen by the largest portion of the site's membership as well as other visitors.

Disqus (www.disqus.com) - Disqus is a comment system and moderation tool for your site. This service lets you add next-gen community management and social web integration to any site on any platform.

DocStoc (www.docstoc.com) - DocStoc is an online sharing service for documents. Users can view, upload, share and sell documents.

E

EventBrite (www.eventbrite.com) - Eventbrite is a provider of online event management and ticketing services. Eventbrite is free if your event is free. If you sell tickets to your event, Eventbrite collects a fee per ticket.

F

Facebook (www.facebook.com) - Facebook is a social utility that connects people with friends and others who work, study and live around them. Facebook is the largest social network in the world with more than 500 million users.

Firefox (http://www.mozilla.org/projects/firefox/) - Firefox is an open-source web browser. It has emerged as one of the most popular web browsers on the Internet and allows users to customize their browser through the use of third-party extensions.

Flash Mob - A flash mob is a large group of people who assemble suddenly in a public place, perform an unusual and pointless act for a brief time, then quickly disperse. The term *flash mob* is generally applied only to gatherings organized via telecommunications, social media, or viral emails.

Flickr (www.flickr.com) - Flickr is a social network based around online picture sharing. The service allows users to store photos online and then share them with others through profiles, groups, sets and other methods.

Forums - Also known as a message board, a forum is an online discussion site. It originated as the modern equivalent of a traditional bulletin board, and a technological evolution of the dialup bulletin board system.

Foursquare (www.foursquare.com) - Foursquare is a social network in which friends share their locations and connect with others in close psychical proximity to each other. The service uses a system of digital badges to reward players who "checkin" to different types of locations.

G

Google Buzz (www.google.com/buzz) - Google Buzz is a social networking and messaging tool from Google, designed to integrate into the company's web-based email program, Gmail. Users can share links, photos, videos, status messages and comments organized in "conversations" and visible in the user's inbox.

Google Chrome (www.google.com/chrome) - Google Chrome is a free web browser produced by Google that fully integrates into its online search system as well as other applications.

Google Documents (www.docs.google.com) - Google Documents is a group of web-based office applications that includes tools for word processing, presentations and spreadsheet analysis. All documents are stored and edited online and allow multiple people to collaborate on a document in real-time.

Gowalla (www.gowalla.com) - Gowalla is a social network in which friends share their locations and connect with others in close psychical proximity to each other.

Groundswell - A social trend in which people use technologies to get the things they need from each other, rather than from traditional institutions like corporations. (Charlene Li and Josh Bernoff, *Groundswell*, pg. 9)

H

Hashtag - A hashtag is a tag used on the social network Twitter as a way to annotate a message. A hashtag is a word or phrase preceded by a "#". Example: #yourhashtag. Hashtags are commonly used to show that a tweet, a Twitter message, is related to an event or conference.

hi5 (www.hi5.com) - hi5 is a social network focused on the youth market. It is a social entertainment destination, with a focus on delivering a fun and entertainment-driven social experience online to users around the world.

HootSuite (www.hootsuite.com) - HootSuite is a web-based Twitter client. With HootSuite, you can manage multiple Twitter profiles, pre-schedule tweets, and view metrics.

HTML - HyperText Markup Language (HTML) is a programing language for web pages. Think of HTML as the brick-and-mortar of pages on the web -- it provides content and structure while CSS supplies style. HTML has changed over the years and it is on the cusp of its next version: HTML5.

I

Inbound Marketing - Inbound marketing is a style of marketing that essentially focuses on getting found by customers. This sense is related to relationship marketing and Seth Godin's idea of permission marketing. David Meerman Scott recommends that marketers "earn their way in" (via publishing helpful information on a blog etc.) in contrast to outbound marketing where they used to have to "buy, beg, or bug their way in" (via paid advertisements, issuing press releases in the hope they get picked up by the trade press, or paying commissioned sales people, respectively).

Instant Messaging - Instant messaging (IM) is a form of real-time direct text-based communication between two or more people. More advanced instant messaging software clients also allow enhanced modes of communication, such as live voice or video calling.

J

Joomla (www.joomla.org) - Joomla is an content management system (CMS) which enables users to build websites and online applications.

K

Kyte (www.kyte.com) - Kyte is an online and mobile video application that provides video hosting and stream for both recorded and live video feeds.

L

Lifecasting - Lifecasting is a continual broadcast of events in a person's life through digital media. Typically, lifecasting is transmitted through the Internet and can involve wearable technology.

Like - A "Like" is an action that can be made by a Facebook user. Instead of writing a comment for a message or a status update, a Facebook user can click the "Like" button as a quick way to show approval and share the message.

Link Building - Link building is an aspect of search engine optimization in which website owners develop strategies to generate links to their site from other websites with the hopes of improving their search engine ranking. Blogging has emerged as a popular method of link building.

LinkedIn (www.linkedin.com) - LinkedIn is a business-oriented social networking site. Founded in December 2002 and launched in May 2003, it is mainly used for professional networking. As of June 2010, LinkedIn had more than 70 million registered users, spanning more than 200 countries and territories worldwide.

Lurker - A lurker online is a person who reads discussions on a message board, newsgroup, social network, or other interactive system, but rarely or never participates in the discussion.

M

Mashup - A content mashup contains multiple types of media drawn from pre-existing sources to create a new work. Digital mashups allow individuals or businesses to create new pieces of content by combining multiple online content sources.

MySpace (www.myspace.com) - MySpace is a social networking website owned by News Corporation. MySpace became the most popular social networking site in the United States in June 2006 and was overtaken internationally by its main competitor, Facebook, in April 2008.

MyPunchbowl (www.punchbowl.com)   -
MyPunchbowl.com is a social network that facilitates party planning and provides members with ideas, invitations, favors, gift registries, photo/video sharing, and more.

N

News Reader - A news reader allows users to aggregate articles from multiple websites into one place using RSS feeds. The purpose of these aggregators is to allow for a faster and more efficient consumption of information.

Newsvine (www.newsvine.com) - Newsvine is a social news site similar to Digg in which users submit and vote for stories to be shared and read by other members of the community.

O

Opera (www.opera.com) - Opera is an open-source web browser. While not as popular as Firefox, Opera is used as the default browser on some gaming systems and mobile devices.

Orkut (www.orkut.com) - Orkut is a social networking website that is owned and operated by Google. The website is named after its creator, Google employee Orkut Büyükkökten. Although Orkut is less popular in the United States than competitors Facebook and MySpace, it is one of the most visited websites in India and Brazil.

P

Pandora (www.pandora.com) - Pandora is a social online radio station that allows users to create stations based on their favorite artists and types of music.

Permalink - A permalink is an address or URL of a particular post within a blog or website.

Podcast - A podcast, or non-streamed webcast, is a series of digital media files, either audio or video, that are released episodically and often downloaded through an RSS feed.

Posterous (www.posterous.com) - Posterous is a blogging and content syndication platform that allows users to post content from any computer or mobile device by sending an e-mail.

PostRank (www.postrank.com) PostRank monitors and collects social engagement related to content around the web. Essentially it helps publishers understand which type of content promotes sharing on the social web.

Q

Qik (www.qik.com) - Qik is an online video streaming service that lets users to stream video live from their mobile phones to the web.

Quantcast (www.quancast.com) - Quantcast provides website traffic and demographics for websites. The tool is primarily used by online advertisers looking to target specific demographics.

R

Real-Time Search - Real-time search is the method of indexing content being published online into search engine results with virtually no delay.

Reddit (www.reddit.com) - Reddit is similar to Digg and Newsvine. It is a social news site that is built upon a community of users who share and comment on stories.

S

Scribd (www.scribd.com) - Scribd turns document formats such as PDF, Word and PowerPoint into a web document for viewing and sharing online.

Search Engine Optimization - Search Engine Optimization is the process of improving the volume or quality of traffic to a website from search engines via unpaid or organic search traffic.

Second Life (www.secondlife.com) - Second Life is an online virtual world developed by Linden Lab that was launched on June 23, 2003. Users are called "residents" and they interact with each other through avatars. Residents can explore, meet other residents, socialize, participate in individual and group activities, create and trade virtual property and services with one another, and travel throughout the world.

Seesmic (www.seesmic.com) - Seesmic is a popular desktop and mobile social application. Using APIs, Seesmic allows users to share content on social networks such as Twitter and Google Buzz from the same application.

Sentiment- Sentiment is normally referred to as the attitude of user comments related to a brand online. Some social media monitoring tools measure sentiment.

SlideShare (www.slideshare.net) - SlideShare is an online social network for sharing presentations and documents. Users can favorite and embed presentations as well as share them on other social networks such as Twitter and Facebook.

Skype (www.skype.com) - Skype is a free program that allows for text, audio and video chats between users. Additionally, users can purchase plans to receive phone calls through their Skype account.

Social Media - Social media is media designed to be disseminated through social interaction, created using highly accessible and scalable publishing techniques.

Social Media Monitoring - Social media monitoring is a process of monitoring and responding to mentions related to a business that occur in social media.

StumbleUpon (www.stumbleupon.com) - Free web-browser extension which acts as an intelligent browsing tool for discovering and sharing web sites.

T

Tag Cloud - A tag cloud is a visual depiction of user-generated tags, or simply the word content of a site, typically used to describe the content of web sites.

Technorati (www.technorati.com) - Technorati is a popular blog search engine that also provides categories and authority rankings for blogs.

TweetDeck (www.tweetdeck.com) - TweetDeck is an application that connects users with contacts across Twitter, Facebook, MySpace, LinkedIn and more.

Tweetup - A Tweetup is an organized or impromptu gathering of people that use Twitter.

Twitter (www.twitter.com) - Twitter is a platform that allows users to share 140-character-long messages publicly. User can "follow" each other as a way of subscribing to each others' messages. Additionally, users can use the @username command to direct a message towards another Twitter user.

Twitter Search (www.search.twitter.com) - Twitter Search is a search engine operated by Twitter to search for Twitter messages and users in real-time.

Tumblr (www.tumblr.com) - Tumblr lets users share content in the form of a blog. Users can post text, photos, quotes, links, music, and videos from your browser, phone, desktop, or email.

TypePad (www.typepad.com) - TypePad is a free and paid blogging platform similar to Blogger. It

Page151

allows users to host and publish their own blogs.

U

Unconference - An unconference is a facilitated, participant-driven conference centered on a theme or purpose. The term "unconference" has been applied, or self-applied, to a wide range of gatherings that try to avoid one or more aspects of a conventional conference, such as high fees and sponsored presentations.

USTREAM (www.ustream.tv) - USTREAM is a live interactive broadcast platform that enables anyone with an Internet connection and a camera to engage to stream video online.

URL - A URL is most popularly known as the "address" of a web page on the World Wide Web, e.g. http://www.example.com

V

Video Blog - A video blog is a blog the produces regular video content often around the same theme on a daily or weekly basis. An example of a successful video blog is Wine Library TV.

Viddler (www.viddler.com) - Viddler is a popular video sharing site similar to YouTube and Vimeo in which users can upload videos to be hosted online and shared and watched by others.

Vimeo (www.vimeo.com) - Vimeo is a popular video sharing service in which users can upload videos to be hosted online and shared and watched by others. Vimeo user videos are often more artistic and the service does not allow commercial video content.

Viral Marketing - Viral marketing refers to marketing techniques that use pre-existing social networks to produce increases in brand awareness or to achieve other marketing objectives through self-replicating viral processes.

W

Web Analytics - Web analytics is the measurement, collection, analysis and reporting of Internet data for purposes of understanding and optimizing web usage.

Webinar - A webinar is used to conduct live meetings, training, or presentations via the Internet.

Widget - A widget is an element of a graphical user interface that displays an information arrangement changeable by the user, such as a window or text box.

Wiki - A wiki is a website that allows the easy creation and editing of any number of interlinked web pages via a web browser, allowing for collaboration between users.

Wikipedia (www.wikipedia.org) - Wikipedia is a

free, web-based, collaborative, multilingual encyclopedia project supported by the non-profit Wikimedia Foundation. Its 15 million articles (over 3.3 million in English) have been written collaboratively by volunteers around the world, and almost all of its articles can be edited by anyone with access to the site.

WordPress (www.wordpress.com) - WordPress is a content management system and contains blog publishing tools that allow users to host and publish blogs.

X

- - -

Y

Yammer (www.yammer.com) - Yammer is a business communication tool that operates as an internal Twitter-like messaging system for employees within an organization. It is used to provide real-time communication and reduce the need for e-mail.

Yelp (www.yelp.com) - Yelp is a social network and local search website that provides users with a platform to review, rate and discuss local businesses. Over 31 million people access Yelp's website each month, putting it in the top 150 U.S. Internet websites.

YouTube (www.youtube.com) - YouTube is a

video-sharing website on which users can upload, share, and view videos. Three former PayPal employees created YouTube in February 2005. In November 2006, YouTube, LLC was bought by Google Inc. for $1.65 billion, and is now operated as a subsidiary of Google. YouTube is the largest video sharing site in the world.

Z

Zoho (www.zoho.com) - Zoho is a suite of online web applications geared towards business productivity and collaboration.

Zooomr (www.zoomr.com) - Zooomr is an online photo sharing service similar to Flickr.

Other books in the same series

An Amazon best-seller on three continents, *SEO Help: 20 steps to get your website to Google's #1 page* is a practical, step-by-step guide which helps those who optimize their own websites rank them high on the largest search engine in the world.

Electronic versions of these books are available from Mobipocket.com, the Sony Bookstore, all major online eBook retailers as well as www.helpmyseo.com.

Stay informed

David Amerland maintains a blog at
www.helpmyseo.com which he runs entirely on his
own. Stay in touch with what is happening in the
world of SEO and online marketing by paying it a
visit.

About the Author

David Amerland is a British journalist. He cut his teeth in the ELan pages of *The European* and joined the tide of misfits trawling the writing waves of the world when Bob Maxwell's publishing empire crumbled towards the end of the last century. He has, since, been involved in writing, publishing and web development launching a series of companies which have explored each frontier. He gained valuable experience in running corporations by being actively involved with the John Lewis Partnership between 1995 – 2002. He has used that to help guide corporations which range from leading Printing Companies in Greece to international Food Importers. He knows that all this makes him difficult to categorize while keeping him gainfully employed. He has an abiding passion for martial arts, Zen and surfing and looks for the unity of all things in everything he does. If you happen to find it before him be kind enough to let him know.

CPSIA information can be obtained at www.ICGtesting.com
224841LV00002B/130/P

9 781844 819881